" . . . a formidable yet worthwhile and pioneering task in a difficult, unpopular area of disturbed human behavior . . . Interesting, readable, original . . . Of value to begin to understand these age-old complex sexual behaviors."

> Domeena C. Renshaw, M.D.
> *Journal of American Medical Association*

"This is an affliction that affects large numbers of men and women."

> Phil Donahue

"Carnes has pioneered a treatment for sex addiction."

> *USA Today*

"What's significant about the (sexual addiction) concept is that it gives people a label for understanding their very puzzling and destructive patterns of sexual behavior."

> John Grace, therapist
> *St. Paul Pioneer Press/Dispatch*

"Carnes is the acknowledged expert in a field that until recently didn't exist."

> *Philadelphia*

"I just want to say thank you for understanding me. It's the first time that I felt my problem crystallized for me. I not only (speak) as a professional, but as an addict. It's the first step for me."

> Anonymous

OUT OF THE SHADOWS

Understanding Sexual Addiction

Second Edition

Patrick Carnes, Ph.D.

CompCare® Publishers

Library of Congress Cataloging-in-Publication Data

Carnes, Patrick, 1944–
   [Sexual addiction]
   Out of the shadows: understanding sexual addiction / Patrick Carnes,
— 2nd ed.
   Previously published as: The sexual addiction.
   Includes bibliographical references (p. 169) and index.
   ISBN 0-89638-269-9
   1. Sex addiction.   I. Title.
  RC560.S43C38   1992
  616.85'83—dc20   92-9624
                                                CIP

Original cover design by Susan Rinek

Inquiries, orders, and catalog requests should be addressed to
CompCare Publishers
2415 Annapolis Lane
Minneapolis, Minnesota 55441
Call 612-559-4800 or
toll free 800-328-3330

  5   4   3
96 95 94 93

This book is intended as a guide to understanding both the sexual addiction and the Twelve Steps as a means of recovery. Neither the book, its author, nor its publisher endorses any specific Twelve Step group for sexual compulsiveness. Readers are encouraged to investigate thoroughly any such group as to its appropriateness for them.

Contents

Charts and Diagrams

Foreword to the Second Edition

I had given my friend Sherod Miller an early draft of what was to be called *Out of the Shadows*. Sherod, whose organization had published an earlier book of mine, was a respected author, with his *Couples Communication* in seventeen foreign editions. I really wanted his opinion of the manuscript. As we talked over dinner in a Minneapolis hotel, Sherod and I discussed my writing. Yet it became clear that the editorial state of the book was not his concern.

He finally looked at me and said, "Pat, this book is going to change your life."

A shudder of premonition went through me—something that always seems to happen when an inescapable reality in my life is reached. I remember quietly dismissing the significance of Sherod's statement by assuring him that I was prepared to face whatever happened. Ten years later to the month, I can say that nothing—not Sherod's comment or anything else—could have prepared me for what happened. And, yes, the book did transform my life.

The book actually appeared in December 1983, entitled *The Sexual Addiction*. I have never agonized as much over any task before or since. I joked that I really did not know how the book was written. What I meant was that this book came from some quiet place of certitude within me—and, in that sense, it was not about me or any abilities that I might possess. It was more about a truth that would not rest until expressed. I simply gave voice to the perception of sexual pain I saw in struggling people.

Shortly after the book appeared, we began to see that the book needed to be retitled. So much shame existed about the illness that readers found it difficult even to purchase the book with the title *The Sexual Addiction*. Renamed *Out of the Shadows*, with *Understanding Sexual Addiction* as a subtitle, the book began to sell. And with more people reading it, those changes Sherod had talked about began to happen.

First came the mail. The book had tapped into a deep undercurrent of sexual trauma in our culture. People needed to talk about their pain. So they wrote letters. Most wrote because they were grateful. Many were struggling with inadequate resources. That is, these were people in prisons with no help, people who had little Twelve Step support in their communities, and others who needed help and could not find treatment or therapists.

All walks of life were represented in these letters, as well as all kinds of sexual addiction problems. There was the woman whose husband failed to return after he had gone to his office on a Sunday in order "to catch up." She and her eight-year-old daughter found him in a rest room, dead of autoerotic asphyxiation. She wrote that she understood the addiction and how he got there. But her greatest problem now was how to deal with her daughter—the image of her father hanging by his belt in the midst of piles of pornography continued to haunt her.

Another came from the daughter of a sex addict who had died of a heart attack. Her mother and sisters were stunned to find that he was simultaneously married to two other women who also had children. Her agony was about her rage damming up her grief.

A Native American man wrote about how sex addiction can parallel alcoholism on the reservations. As a therapist, an alcoholic, and a recovering sex addict, he wrote with the authority of someone who had been there. He described how young Indian children had been taken out of abusive families and placed in common schools. There they were sexually abused by the older children, and the older ones were, in turn, being abused by the staff. As he wrote, "It was no accident I ended up where I did." His efforts to advocate for kids were, at best, met by apathy and more often by outrage by government agencies and even by the tribal council. The good news is that his individual voice—unwelcome as it was—made a difference.

I heard from a professional, who told this painful story. In the early '80s, his exhibitionism was so bad that he knew it was only a matter of time before his arrest. He so feared how this would affect his wife and children that he plotted his suicide. He had tried all the therapies available and felt there were no alternatives for him. So he took out large insurance policies and planned a car "accident." Filled with pain and suicidal, he spotted a copy of *Out of the Shadows*. It offered enough hope for him to seek a Twelve Step group and therapy. Seven years later, he has over six years of problem-free behavior, a successful career, and a supportive family. He thinks about the old days in the street only about twice a year. And, when he does, whatever power the compulsion still has is overwhelmed by gratitude.

Then there were the letters from the elderly. One woman told me that her husband, who himself was a therapist, discovered the book a few months before he died. She said it was "like gold" to him. Knowing about the addiction brought him peace. Similarly, another woman wrote about how her husband had been disabled by a car accident when he was fifty-four, just as she was about to leave him because of his womanizing. Because he was an invalid, she instead chose to stay with him. Upon his death twenty years later, she was amazed to find two decades of letters written since the accident to women she did not know about. Finding *Out of the Shadows* helped her separate her grief over the loss of a loved one from that other grief that comes with feeling betrayed.

Out of the Shadows started a conversation about the dark side of our sexuality. In the early struggle to educate people about alcoholism, we had to deal mostly with extreme prejudice, ignorance, and pain. The subject of sex addiction, however, tapped into some of our most primitive terrors. The reactions to it, therefore, are exponential. Unlike alcohol, sex is at the core of our identities. To understand our sexuality in new ways forces shifts in our self-perceptions.

All suffering contains gifts. And sex addiction is no different. It has expanded dramatically our knowledge of addictions in general. As a result of our increasing awareness of sex addiction, we know more about the addictive family system, the neurochemistry of addictions, the role of child abuse in addictions, and the impact of shame on addictive behavior. As eating disorders have helped us understand healthy eating, so sex addiction has provided us with new perspectives on healthy sex. The women's movement, the men's movement, pornography, AIDS, sex offenders, sexual harrassment—many of our most divisive or controversial issues are sexual ones, and they take on new shades of meaning within the context of sex addiction.

Sex addiction itself has not been without controversy. But the debate has shifted from concerns about whether or not such an illness exists, to how, and in what forms, and for what reasons.

Sex addicts have taught me much since *Out of the Shadows* was written. My book *Don't Call It Love* (Bantam, 1991), describes the course of recovery for over a thousand sex addicts and their partners. These books are very different. The science of the second simply validates the spirit of the first.

Among the many realities for sex addicts that *Out of the Shadows* describes and *Don't Call It Love* verifies is the reality of child abuse as a causal factor. In fact, our research showed that the more severely you were abused sexually and physically as a child, the more addictions you had as an adult. Eighty-one percent of addicts—the figure applies both to men and to women—had been sexually abused. Seventy-two percent had been physically abused. How severely sex addicts were abused emotionally serves as a predictor of who will abuse children in the next generation.

Based on the *Don't Call It Love* research and the large number of hospital admissions, we know that sex addiction usually accompanies other addictions, like chemical dependency (42 percent) and eating disorders (38 percent). In fact, out of a pool of four thousand sex addicts, less than thirteen percent reported having just the one addiction.

We also were able to document the kinds of families sex addicts tend to come from. First, they are families with little cohesion, so not much emotional bonding occurs. Many addicts value *Out of the Shadows* because it has helped them understand the role of abandonment in their addictive process. Second, sex addicts tend to come from rigid, autocratic families with extremely high standards of behavior. To vary from the norms would bring harsh judgment and criticism. This intense criticism is one of the key factors in shame—and shame underlies all addictions, but especially sexual addiction.

One of the most important learnings of our research is about addicts' co-addicted partners. In every descriptive category—such as child abuse experiences, family characteristics, life problems, and coping styles—the percentages were the same for the co-addict as for the addict. For example, eighty-one percent of both addicts and co-addicts were abused sexually as children. Research simply confirmed that addicts were part of a family "system."

We have learned many things since the first publication of *Out of the Shadows*. We know now, for instance, that an addict and a co-addict will go through definite stages of recovery over five years. These stages are predictable, almost to the month. Despite such learnings, we have not changed the basic text of this book. We thought it better to preserve the quality of what it does best—help those who are beginning recovery to understand their illness. When their commitment to their recovery deepens, they can learn more as they are ready.

I work now with a sexual dependency program at Del Amo Hospital in Torrance, California. We are using technology I had not even imagined ten years ago to help sex addicts and sexual trauma patients. Professional colleagues in hospitals and outpatient settings all over the nation are doing creative and innovative therapy. Professionals can share their progress at national conferences on sex addiction. We now have the National Council on Sex Addiction, an organization that pulls together concerned citizens, recovering people, and committed professionals to help the public understand the nature of this illness (see the new, updated Resource Guide on page 177). I had not a glimmer of all this a decade ago.

The driving force for these changes comes from recovering people themselves. It is the transformations in their lives that have helped to educate the professionals and convince the critics. Theirs are stories of great courage.

I know two men who started a Twelve Step group in a southern state. After confiding to each other about their problem, one decided to go to treatment, and the other put the word out that they were beginning a Twelve Step meeting. For six Sunday evenings, the latter went alone to the church meeting room, set up the chairs, waited, and prayed. No one came. When the man returned from treatment and came to the meeting, a third member showed up. Now that meeting has grown so large that it has split many times and has developed wonderful traditions as a Twelve Step community. It all grew out of the faith of one and the action of the other. And so it has happened all over the country.

Yet the significance of this increasing understanding of sex addiction is more than the impact of individual stories, dramatic and encouraging as they are. There are those who make a case that the conflict, competition, and exploitation that erode our planet will not change until we, as humans, move into more collaborative and cooperative modes. Such a change in ecology starts with the most fundamental aspect of our relationships: our sexuality. We cannot evolve further until men and women treat each other differently. Respect for sexual preference, the protection of children from inappropriate and abusive behavior, the reduction of sexual shame, and the celebration of sexual joy will emerge naturally with a shift to nonpatriarchal, noncompetitive, and nonexploitive values about sex.

Each sex addict's recovery, therefore, is a clear contribution to the well-being of the planet. Sex addicts know how that recovery begins. For every addict a moment comes. . .

Patrick J. Carnes, Ph.D.
The Sexual Dependency Program
Del Amo Hospital
Torrance, California

Preface

This book represents an extraordinary pilgrimage for me. It started as an extended paper I wrote early in 1976 entitled, "The Sex Offender: His Addiction, His Family, His Beliefs." Based on two years of experience of conducting outpatient groups with sex offenders, the paper developed the essential concepts that underlie this book and its companion volume, *Contrary to Love, Understanding Sexual Addiction, Part 2: Helping the Sexual Addict.*

The manuscript received wide circulation, but was never published. The paper served as a basis for many workshops and training events. Whole programs evolved based on its theoretical assumptions. Yet, I remained reluctant to make the document a formal statement through publication. One reason for the reluctance was the realization that the sexual addiction extended to many men and women who had not done anything punishable by law. They were not "sex offenders," but suffered the same pathology. Also, in those early years there was insufficient documentation to support the concept of sexual compulsiveness as an addiction. Nor were there networks of programs available to help people who recognized their need. Most of all, I was afraid of the public reaction which is always unpredictable in sexual matters. In short, it was an idea whose time had not come.

In 1976, a suburban hospital asked me to start an experimental program for chemically dependent families. Called the Family Renewal Center, the program required that all members of the family above age six participate in the 330-hour program. The theoretical constructs of the program originated in general systems theory, especially as it applied to families and the Twelve Steps of Alcoholics Anonymous. Within a short time, the entire staff realized that having all the family members present in the therapeutic process radically altered one's understanding of alcoholism and chemical dependency.

One of the many factors which stood out from a family perspective was that the addictive compulsivity had many forms other than alcohol and drug abuse. Also, the different forms— overeating, gambling, sexuality, buying, shoplifting—all shared a similar process. And in addition, within the family, addictions would be like overlays whose reinforcing shadows simply deepened the patterns of family pathology.

To further complicate matters, the reactions of family members to the multi-addiction patterns were as unhealthy as the coping of the addicts themselves. In understanding the family illness, we learned that each member must use a discipline such as the Twelve Steps as an on-going antidote to the addictive process. Members of groups like Overeaters Anonymous and Gamblers Anonymous had already pioneered in applying the Twelve Steps to other addictions. Now the Family Renewal Center has extended its programming, based on the Twelve Steps, to sexual addiction, physical abuse, and food issues. The center also offers a series of wellness programs for families and couples.

Other than its offerings in chemical dependency, the center's sexual addiction programs are the most developed series of programs at the center. Sexual compulsivity was the first of the "other" addictions we tackled by virtue of continuing my outpatient group work with offenders. Program development was intensified with a three-year grant from the National Center on Child Abuse and Neglect. Now the center offers family-oriented sexual abuse programs both in urban and rural sites and other similar programs are being set up in other regions of the country. The research efforts of that staff are, to my knowledge, the first extended and systematic articulation of the relationship between sexual compulsivity and chemical dependency that has a sound empirical base. Data and experience now exist which add credibility to the conceptualization done so many years ago.

Also, the growth of Twelve Step programs for sexual addiction across the country is a most encouraging development. The emerging network of groups not only provides help to people in pain, it also represents a milestone of public support, without which sexual addicts will never ultimately be able to escape their shame.

Over the years, the many discussions I have had with my colleagues and friends have made it difficult to isolate the genesis of concepts. I am indebted to them all for their contributions. Especially, I wish to thank:

Miriam Ingebritson, whose creativity and critiques have often expanded my own limited paradigms.

Glenice Anderson, Dave Walsh, Tom Burton, Craig Nakken, Jim Michel, Shirley Carlson, Mary McBride, and the staff of the Family Renewal Center, whose advice, integrity, and support have been invaluable.

Allen Nohre, executive director of Fairview Treatment Centers, for his continuing support of my work.

Bill Mease, Warren Shaffer, Mark Davison, Richard Seely, Scott Moline, and Elaine Pfalzgraf, who as legal, police, or psychological professionals made important resources available.

Ann Golla and Janis Kromminga, who spent many long evening and weekend hours typing the manuscripts.

The members of Sexual Addicts Anonymous (SAA) whose reading and suggestions were the real test.

Professor Richard Clendenen and the alumni of the Juvenile Officers Institute of the University of Minnesota—if they had not confronted me, I would never have finished this book.

Diane DuCharme, whose early encouragement was indispensable.

Bonnie Hesse, who as editor could not have been more affirming.

Terri, my wife, whose patient editing, care, and commitment sustain all my writing.

My children, David, Stefanie, Jennifer, and Erin, who have explained to me that this is one book they will not bring to school.

The people whose stories are reflected in these pages and who are the true pioneers.

With all of these people, my pilgrimage has not been alone and for that I am truly grateful. With their help, what was begun in 1976 is now finished.

Introduction

A Moment Comes for Every Addict

A moment comes for every addict when the consequences are so great or the pain is so bad that the addict admits life is out of control because of his or her sexual behavior. Some are newsmaking moments such as the public censure when a congressman, minister, or professional figure is cited for unacceptable sexual behavior. Millions read the steamy news accounts and despite their own prurience make severe judgments about people who are sexual with children, who visit prostitutes, who commit homosexual acts in public toilets, or who even have affairs. A smaller audience—but much larger than most imagine—read each line fearing that the same public exposure could happen to them and judging themselves with the same unforgiving standards the public uses.

Some are dramatic moments, like:

- When the squad car pulls into the driveway and you know why they've come...
- When you break off yet another relationship you never wanted to be in...
- When your spouse announces the end of your marriage because of the latest discovery...
- When your daughter's friend sees your picture in the mug shots at the police station and no one in your family knew...
- When you have to leave your job because of a sexual entanglement with a person you never really liked anyway...
- When your teenage son finds your pornography...
- When the school counselor calls to inform you that your daughter does not want to come home because, after eight years, she does not want to be sexual anymore, and you are being reported to child protection...
- When you have a car accident while exposing yourself.

Some are secret moments known only to yourself, like:

- When you have to tell yet another lie which you almost believe yourself...
- When the money you have spent on the last prostitute equals the amount for the new shoes your child needs...
- When you see a person on the street you had been sexual with in a restroom...
- When you make business travel decisions not on the basis of the company interests, but rather the affair that you are having...
- When you tell someone "I love you," knowing full well there are two others who also think they are the only ones you love...
- When you sit in a room full of people, three of whom you have made love with recently. Part of you fears what they would do if they knew, and part of you gloats over your accomplishment...
- When you say "I love you" because you know you are going to go to bed with someone. Yet you really don't love him, nor do you want to go to bed with him...
- When you cringe inside because your friends are laughing at a flasher joke, and you are one...
- When you are an alcoholic completing treatment and you realize that your time in the hospital was not only a period free from chemicals, but also a time when you were sexually at ease as well, and you never felt better. You know, however, that sobriety will be easy compared to stopping your sexual addiction.

For most people these moments are followed by resolves "never to do it again." Even as the promises are made, they are rendered hollow by the echoes of the previous vows and resolutions. Many are the addicts who have deeply wished just not to be sexual, thinking that to be the only cure for their compulsive feelings, thinking that by giving up their *sexuality* they would be able to work, to love, and to enjoy themselves like other people. Sexual addiction has been described as "the athlete's foot of the mind." It never goes away. It always is asking to be scratched, promising relief. To scratch, however, is to cause pain and to intensify the itch.

The "itch" is created in part by the rationalizations, lies, and beliefs about themselves carried deep within the sexual addicts. The husband, for example, who visits a prostitute and on his way home feels warmly towards his wife and family, tells himself that his time in the sauna really helps him to be more sensitive and loving to his family. At one level he knows the fallacy of his thinking, but chooses to ignore it in light of the immediate warm feelings. In contrast with the unfeeling exchanges of massage parlor life, the family does look much better. The cost to the family remains overlooked, however. So it is with the many beliefs, rationalizations, and myths which support addiction:

I am oversexed.
No one else is like me.
I really did care for her/him.
Just one more time won't hurt.
I deserve it.
It isn't so bad since everyone does it.
She/he wanted, deserved, asked for it.

One of the greatest myths which allows the addict to repeat sexual behaviors is that it does not adversely affect other relationships, especially a marriage. In fact, one of the most common rationales for a married addict is that "I do it in order to stay in the marriage." In reality, though, the marriage is often characterized by diminishing intimacy, sensitivity, and sexuality. The corollary myth is that the family does not know about the secret sexual life. Yet, at one level, they always do know...even the children.

The facts are that—like all addictions—the sexual addiction is also rooted in a complex web of family and marital relationships. This interdependent web is truly a system in which a number of things act together to form one function, like a biological system or even a computer system. The system is governed by definite rules which, in the addict's case, confirm much of what he or she holds to be true in the crazy myths and beliefs which support the addiction. Also, all member parts have a functional relationship; that is, each person affects every other person. Nothing happens in isolation in this or any other system.

For the addict, part of therapy is to discover the role of the previous generation in the addiction. The exhibitionist who learns that his father, two uncles, and two cousins were also exhibitionists becomes keenly aware of how the "sins" of one generation are visited upon the next. Yet, for years he was convinced he was the only one afflicted with the compulsion—a myth which added to the shame and pain at the core of his addiction. Many addicts find that the patterns of compulsion are learned quite early in the form of abuse, seduction, or simply witnessing compulsiveness in others.

Family members too have their parts in the system. The spouse who has learned that her husband has been sexual with every one of her close friends cancels travel plans to visit her family because he might do it again. A husband seeks out his wife's latest lover in an effort to stop their relationship. A wife buys her husband marijuana, which she hates to do, but rationalizes that it is better to have him numb on the couch than out exposing himself or chasing another woman. These people have in common the belief that it is in their power to stop the spouse's addiction. That is where their delusion begins and as a result they become obsessed with their spouse's compulsive behavior. Ironically, efforts to control the spouse's behavior unwittingly intensify the addiction process.

Because our sexuality is one of our most fundamental life processes, sexual compulsiveness is extremely threatening to all of us. The intensity of our fears can be easily measured by the complex mosaic of proscriptions, laws, and taboos we use to guide our sexual behavior. This mosaic is the real expression of our values and cultural wisdom. When someone breaks a sexual taboo, i.e., goes beyond the socially acceptable limit, everyone's trust is shaken in our most fundamental social bonds—those "rules," written or commonly understood, which allow us as individuals to live comfortably with each other as a society.

While our society is shifting to a more open attitude toward sexual expression, we still view the amount and kind of activity as a matter of personal choice. For the addict, however, there is no choice. No choice. The addiction is in charge. That addicts have no control over their sexual behavior is a very hard concept to accept when the addicts' trails have left broken marriages and parentless children, or worse, victims of sexual crimes. Therefore, there are no neutral responses to sexual compulsivity.

Addicts, at one level, judge themselves by society's standards. Unable to live up to these, they live with constant pain and alienation. Each one, convinced that he or she alone is afflicted, lives in isolation and constant fear of discovery. Addicts withhold a major portion of themselves—a pain deeply felt, but never expressed nor witnessed. They do not trust nor do they become intimate with others—especially their families. There is the possibility family members will find out about their behavior and the certainty that they will leave the addicts. As we shall see, fear of abandonment and shame are at the core of addiction. The alienation becomes a quagmire within which addicts struggle only to become more isolated.

Family members too become more isolated as the addiction progresses. Their lives are filled with secret concerns about themselves and their family. Their worst fear is also discovery. What if what they suspect is true? What if something else

happens? Spouses wonder about their attractiveness and sexuality and they also fear abandonment and public ridicule. Children worry that the family problems are their fault. The sum
total of the apprehension means that the family members end
up feeling lonely, keeping secrets, and hurting. The obvious is
ignored in the hopes it will disappear, and the family sinks
deeper. Their efforts to struggle free also mire them even more
quickly.

For both the addict and the family members, there is a way
out. The Twelve Steps of Alcoholics Anonymous and Al-Anon
have been a successful path to recovery for millions whose
addiction was alcohol. The same process works for sexual addiction, providing a program by which one can live on a daily
basis, short-circuiting that awful cycle in which what someone
does to relieve pain makes him hurt even more. No longer do
the sexual addicts and family members need to be alone with
their illness. The Steps provide a process through which they
can forgive themselves, make amends, and receive support for
non-compulsive behavior.

If you are an addict or suspect you are and have the courage
to face yourself, this book is intended for you. If you are a
family member or concerned person, this book will also require
courage and honesty, for it is about you as well. For the reader
who, for whatever reason, finds it important to read this book,
you too will have to struggle with your own beliefs and assumptions as you begin to appreciate our society's role in the addict's
pain.

Ultimately, what is written here is about hope. By the reader's
recognition of what happens in the addict's life, the isolation
is, in fact, broken. The secret of the sexual addiction is out—
people are not alone with the problem. Moreover the Twelve
Steps are a concrete, proven path out of the quagmire.

In reading this book, there are some things to remember.
First, addiction taps into the most fundamental human proces-

ses. Whether the need is to be high, to be sexual, to eat, or even to work—the addictive process can turn creative, life-giving energy into a destructive, demoralizing compulsivity. The central losses are the addict's values and relationships. The phenomenon of multiple addictions is not surprising, given the pervasive nature of addiction. Overweight, overwork, and alcoholism are often part of the addict's life. So, in many ways, the book is a statement about the nature of addiction.

Also, the stories used in this book are fictionalized composites based on hundreds of First Step and Fourth Step preparations. They are carefully designed to be characterizations in order to protect individual anonymity. To the degree that they represent any individual is a comment on the commonality of the addicts' experiences. It may be even a greater indicator of how much we all—including non-addicts—are part of the problem.

Please note, when I have chosen to use he and him as pronouns, it has been simply in order to preserve sentence continuity. This is with apology and full recognition to those women who have struggled so painfully with their addiction. Throughout the book, attention is given to the plight of women addicts. Their courage truly needs to be acknowledged.

For the professional who is looking for theoretical and empirical foundations, footnotes are collected for each chapter at the end of the book. For further information look to the companion volume. In it is a history of how the concepts of sexual addiction were developed including case histories, treatment planning, and intervention strategies. The issues in the companion book are of particular interest to counselors, judges, probation officers, and other professionals. However, this book is an effort to provide a non-technical statement for anyone—addict, family member, and other concerned persons—to appreciate the nature and magnitude of the addict's problem and how the Twelve Steps can be a path to recovery out of sexual compulsivity.

Finally, this book is written to help the many addicts who have been afraid to admit their pain. One of the strongest bonds of the addiction is its secrecy. Perhaps, with the secret broken, addicts can know the peace and self-acceptance that comes with knowing *it can be talked about.*

1

The Addiction Cycle

Although Hefner was approaching forty-five, and had been involved with hundreds of photogenic women since starting his magazine, he enjoyed female companionship now more than ever; and perhaps more significant, considering all that Hefner had seen and done in recent years, was the fact that each occasion with a new woman was for him a novel experience. It was as if he was always watching for the first time a woman undress, rediscovering with delight the beauty of the female body, breathlessly expectant as panties were removed and smooth buttocks were exposed – and he never tired of the consummate act. He was a sex junkie with an insatiable habit.

Gay Talese
Thy Neighbor's Wife

Del was a lawyer. Brilliant, charming, and witty. He had a special breakthrough in his career when he was appointed as one of the governor's special aides. His wife and three children were proud of his accomplishments. However, Del's public visibility was creating a problem because he was also a sexual addict. His double life included prostitution, porno bookstores, and affairs.

Del would initiate relationships with women, feeling that he was "in love." After the initial sexual contact, he would desperately wish to be free. These relationships became characterized by his ambivalence. He wanted to be sexual, but he did not want the relationship. Yet he couldn't say no clearly without fear of hurting the women's feelings, so he never quite broke off the relationships. Instead he hoped their frustration would force them to give up. The result was that he had a series of relationships at the same time in various stages of initiation and frustration.

There was not only the juggling act of keeping his relationships straight. Some of these women were vital to him professionally. He exploited relationships to receive cooperation. His problem was that the women would believe that he cared for them. The professional complications were extreme. One time, he was involved with a colleague and her secretary at the same time. The secretary went in to talk to her boss about this ''problem'' she had. Del had to face two very angry women.

His other behaviors were also problems. In porno shops, he was sexual with a number of men in the movie booths. Worse, the shops he frequented were near the capitol where he was liable to be recognized. He vowed to stop when, sitting in a meeting in the attorney general's office, a plan was described for a raid on a local porno shop—the one he had patronized two days before. But he did not stop.

Neither were his visits to massage parlors without peril. One night his masseuse was a young girl quite high on some form of drug. Del decided to have his massage anyway, including a ''hand job.'' When she masturbated him, she hurt his penis. Del was too shameful to complain or even to tell anybody. When he got home, he was so upset, he masturbated—despite his penis being sore.

Late one evening, Del pulled up next to a young woman at a stoplight. He had always had the fantasy of picking up a woman on a street. He looked at her and she smiled at him. Del became very excited. They drove side by side for several blocks. She returned his stares at each stop sign. Soon she pulled ahead of him, turned off the road, and pulled to a stop. He followed and pulled up behind her. She waved towards him and pulled out again. Del thought she wanted him to follow.

Del's mind raced ahead to where she could be leading him. She drove in the direction of a well-known local restaurant with a popular late night bar. Convinced that was where they headed, he speculated that after a drink, they might end up at her apartment. His mind filled with fantasies, he pulled up behind her when she stopped. As he was opening his door, she leaped out of her car and dashed into the building. Surprised, he looked up to see that he was not in front of the restaurant. Rather, she had stopped at the police station three blocks away.

Horrified, Del got back in his car and raced home. While driving, he was in shock at how out of touch with reality he was. She had not been encouraging him to follow her, but was in fact frightened. He, on the other hand, was so caught up in his fantasy, he failed to notice that she was parking at a police station.

He felt a flood of remorse for subjecting the woman to a frightening ordeal. Also, he was terrified that she would accuse him of attempted rape and that he would be arrested. When Del arrived home at 1:30 a.m., he was so scared that he sat and prayed. At 2:00, there was a sound of a siren in the distance. He promised God that he would change. He fantasized about what it would do to his wife and kids. Truly, it was the most desperate moment of his life. Finally, he went to bed.

When he awoke in the morning, he felt tremendous relief. He knew he was not to be picked up. He went to work and put enormous energy into his job that day. At the end of the day, he felt the need of a reward. He stopped at a massage parlor.

Del was a man who valued the law. He also prided himself on his honesty with people—a fact he often parlayed into seduction. His children and wife were central to his life. He had worked hard in his career. His addiction, however, violated his own values and the law, as well as jeopardized his career and family. His story – of which just a few pieces are related here – is one of constant predicaments. Del's addictive behavior put

3

him in situations in which he was vulnerable to tremendous consequences. His degradation was only exceeded by the violation of his own principles. Because of Del's sexual addiction, his fantasy became more real than the nightmare he created.

What Is Sexual Addiction?

A way to understand sexual addicts like Del is to compare them with other types of addicts. A common definition of alcoholism or drug dependency is that a person has a pathological relationship with a mood-altering chemical.[1] The alcoholic's relationship with alcohol becomes more important than family, friends, and work. The relationship progresses to the point where alcohol is necessary to feel normal. To feel "normal" for the alcoholic is also to feel isolated and lonely since the primary relationship he depends upon to feel adequate is a chemical, not other people.

The sexual addiction is parallel. The addict substitutes a sick relationship to an event or process for a healthy relationship with others. The addict's relationship with a mood-altering "experience" becomes central to his life. Del, for example, routinely jeopardized all that he loved. His vows to quit were lost against the power of his addiction. The only thing which exceeded his pain was his loneliness.

Addicts progressively go through stages in which they retreat further from the reality of friends, family, and work. Their secret lives become more real than their public lives. What people know is a false identity. Only the individual addict knows the shame of living a double life—the real world and the addict's world.

Leading a fantasy double life is a distortion of reality. Del was so caught up in his fantasy a police station became a restaurant and a cooperative prospect was, in fact, a desperate

4

and frightened woman. An essential part of sanity is being grounded in reality, so in the sense that addicts distort reality, the sexual addiction becomes a form of insanity.

The Addict's Belief System

How does addiction begin? How does the progressive insanity occur? It begins with the delusional thought processes which are rooted in the addict's *belief system*. That is, addicts begin with core beliefs about themselves which affect how they perceive reality. So important is this factor—the belief system—in the addiction equation, it is a theme throughout this entire book. For now, we need only to point out its role in the impaired thinking of the addict.

Each person has a belief system which is the sum of the assumptions, judgments, and myths that one holds to be true. It contains potent family messages about a person's value or worth, relationships, needs and sexuality. Within it is a repertoire of what "options"—answers, solutions, methods, possiblities, ways of behaving—are open to each of us. In short, it is a model of the world.

On the basis of that model we:

> plan and make decisions.
> interpret other people's actions.
> make meaning out of life experiences.
> solve problems.
> pattern our relationships.
> develop our careers.
> establish priorities.

For each of us, our belief system is the filter through which we conduct the main task of our lives: making choices.

The addict's belief system contains certain core beliefs which are faulty or inaccurate and, consequently, which provide a fundamental momentum for the addiction. Generally, addicts do not perceive themselves as worthwhile persons. Nor do they believe other people would care for them or meet their needs if everything was known about them, including the addiction. Finally, they believe that sex is their most important need. Sex is what makes isolation bearable. Their core beliefs are the anchor points of the sexual addiction.

Impaired Thinking

Out of the belief system—the set of interacting faulty beliefs— come distorted views of reality. Denial leads the list of ways addicts distort reality. Addicts use many devices to deny—to themselves and others—that there is a problem. Ignoring the problem, blaming others, and minimizing the behaviors are part of the addict's defensive repertoire. Consequences such as venereal disease, unwanted pregnancy, lost jobs, arrests, and broken relationships are either overlooked or attributed to factors other than the addiction:

Venereal disease	—"A lot of people get it now."
Pregnancy	—"She tricked me into it."
Arrests	—"Cops had it in for me. They had no real proof."
Jobs	—"The boss needs to be liberated."
Relationships	—"Her family always had problems. She simply couldn't handle it."

When addicts believe in the defensive rationalizations, the result is *denial* that a specific incident or behavior is a part of a total behavioral pattern.

Arguments, excuses, justifications, and circular reasoning abound in the addict's impaired mental processes:

If I don't have it every few days, the pressure builds up.
I am oversexed and have to meet my needs.
What she doesn't know won't hurt.
She really enjoyed, asked for, deserved it.
Every guy will get what "nookie" he can.
If only my wife would be more responsive.
Men are like animals—males are more sexual
    than females.
With the stress I am under, I deserve it.
It doesn't hurt anybody because . . .
I couldn't help it, given how she acted.
No one really cares.
It's my way of relaxing.
Women always pretend they don't want it when
    they do.

Whatever the *rationalization*, it further cuts the addicts off from the reality of their behavior.

Sincere delusion is believing your own lies. The addicts who make a commitment to change or follow through on something are sincere in their intentions. They are as sincere as when they vow to themselves to quit. They may even experience a great deal of emotion—tears of pain, expressions of tenderness, or anger when someone doesn't believe in their good intentions. However, their commitment to others is no more valid than their vows to themselves. It appears to be paradoxical to be sincere about telling a lie. It is not. But it is evidence of seriously impaired thinking.

An example of the thinking process will help. The addict who has been confronted by his wife because he was not at work when he was suppose to be spins out a tale as to his whereabouts. She doubts he is telling the truth. He is incensed at her distrust. He assumes she would be this way even if he were truthful. So he takes it a step further. He assures her that he had even told her earlier that this would happen. This makes her feel even crazier, because she cannot remember. His emotions about her distrust are real. He is now even more incensed that she cannot remember. His lies and his sincerity become fused.

Making declarations of love in order to seduce, becoming incensed at the behavior of the arresting officer in order to obscure your own behavior, and protesting that something "happened only once" in order to cover up—all are types of sincere delusion.

Ironically, the addict knows that he really is *not* trustworthy. In his isolation, he is also convinced that most people cannot be trusted. Further, he is certain that if anyone found out about his secret life of addictive experiences, there would be no forgiveness. Only judgment. To complicate matters, he has placed himself in so many precarious situations, he lives in constant fear of discovery of his being so untrustworthy. The *suspicion* and *paranoia* heighten the sense of alienation.

The addict's blame of others for all problems is another way to protect his secret life. Fault lies with spouse, children, parents, work associates, or boss. The addict is critical, self-righteous, and judgmental. There is no acceptance of personal responsibility for mistakes, failures, or actions. This appearance of integrity further insulates the addict's world from reality. The *blame dynamic* provides further justification for the addict's behavior. Ungrateful children, demanding spouses, hard-nosed bosses create an unfair world in which the addict deserves a reward. To be honest about one's limitations would bring the wall crumbling down—and, in turn, jeopardize the one source of nurturing and care that can be counted on: the sexual addiction.

Each of these delusional thought processes—denial, rationalization, sincere delusion, paranoia, and blame—closes off an important avenue of self-knowledge and touch with reality for the addict. Gone are the feedback loops which serve as vital correctives to a faulty belief system. In this way the addict's world becomes closed off from the real world. Within that world the addictive cycle is now free to work.

The Addiction Cycle

For sexual addicts an addictive experience progresses through a four-step cycle which intensifies with each repetition:

1. *Preoccupation*—the trance or mood wherein the addicts' minds are completely engrossed with thoughts of sex. This mental state creates an obsessive search for sexual stimulation.

2. *Ritualization*—the addicts' own special routines which lead up to the sexual behavior. The ritual intensifies the preoccupation, adding arousal and excitement.

3. *Compulsive sexual behavior*—the actual sexual act, which is the end goal of the preoccupation and ritualization. Sexual addicts are unable to control or stop this behavior.

4. *Despair*—the feeling of utter hopelessness addicts have about their behavior and their powerlessness.

The pain the addicts feel at the end of the cycle can be numbed or obscured by sexual preoccupation which re-engages the addiction cycle.

Sexual addicts are hostages of their own *preoccupation.* Every passerby, every relationship, and every introduction to someone passes through the sexually obsessive filter. More than merely noticing sexually attractive people, there is a quality of desperation which interferes with work, relaxation, and even sleep. People become objects to be scrutinized. A walk through a crowded downtown area is translated into a veritable shopping list of "possibilities."

To understand the trance-like state of preoccupation imagine the intense passion of courtship. We laugh at two lovers who are so absorbed in one another that they forget about their surroundings. The *intoxication* of young love is what the addict attempts to capture. It is the pursuit, the hunt, the search, the suspense heightened by the unusual, the stolen, the forbidden, the illicit which are intoxicating to the sexual addict. The new conquest of the hustler, the score of the exposer, voyeur, or rapist, or the temptation of breaking the taboo of sex with one's child—in essence, they are variations of a theme: courtship gone awry.

The addict uses—or abuses, rather—one of the most exciting moments in human experience: sex. Sexual arousal becomes intensified. The addict's mood is altered as he or she enters the obsessive trance. The metabolic responses are like a rush through the body as adrenaline speeds up the body's functioning. The heart pounds as the addict focuses on his search object. Risk, danger, and even violence are the ultimate escalators. One can always increase the dosage of intoxication. Preoccupation effectively buries the personal pain of remorse or regret. The addict does not always have to act. Often just thinking about it brings relief.

The sexual addict's excitement-seeking parallels some other types of compulsive/obsessive addicts. In that sense, there is little difference between the voyeur waiting for hours by a window for ninety seconds of nudity and the compulsive gambler hunching on a long shot. What makes the sexual addict different is that he draws upon the human emotions generated by courtship and passion.

The trance is enhanced by the sexual addict's *ritualization*. Professionals have often wondered why sex offenders use the same "MO" (*modus operandi* or method) each time, when it only makes apprehension easier. The answer is simple. A ritual helps the trance. Like a yogi in meditation, the addict does not have to stop and think or disrupt his focus. The ritual itself, like preoccupation, can start the rush of excitement.

Addicts often talk about their rituals. The compulsive masturbator and his surroundings, the incestuous father and his elaborate preparations, the exposer's regular routes, the hustler's approach and cruising area—all involve complex rituals. The rituals contain a set of well-rehearsed cues which trigger arousal.

The preoccupation trance supported by extensive rituals is as important as—or sometimes more important than—sexual contact or orgasm. The intoxication of the whole experience is what the addict seeks in order to move through the cycle from despair to exhilaration. One cannot be orgasmic all the time. So the search and the suspense absorb the addict's concentration and energy. Cruising, watching, waiting, preparing are part of the mood alteration.

The first two phases of the addictive cycle (preoccupation and ritualization) are not always visible. The addict struggles to present an image of normalcy to the outside world. The public self is a false ego, since the addict knows the incongruity of his double life. Compulsive sexual behavior, the third phase of the cycle, however, leaves a trail, despite the protective public image.

In the story of Del, described earlier in this chapter, Del repeatedly made commitments to himself and to God that he would stop. These resolves were short-lived. Del could not control his behavior even though he wanted to. Like Del, addicts are *powerless* over their behavior. They have lost control over their sexual expression—which is exactly why they are defined as *addicts*. The failure of their efforts to control their behavior is a sign of their addiction. Sexual addicts often describe the process of picking a day—a child's birthday, a change of jobs, a holiday—as "the last day." Usually, this marks a time when "it" will never happen again. Sometimes addicts will set goals—a year, a month, or a week. Whether forever or a shorter time, the addicts betray themselves, buying into the delusion that they are in control of their behavior. When they fail, yet another indictment of self-control and morality is added to ever-increasing shame. For the recovering addicts who have acknowledged powerlessness, there is hope. They know that they might get through one day free from their addiction—with a lot of help.

The *despair* which the addict experiences after being compulsively sexual is the "low" phase of the four-step cycle. The let-down combines the sense of failure at not having lived up to resolutions to stop with hopelessness about ever being able to stop. If the behavior was particularly degrading, humiliating, or risky, the addict's self-pity grows. If the behavior violated basic personal values or exploited them, the addict experiences self-hatred as well. Addicts often report suicidal feelings along with their despair and shame.

Standing in the wings, however, is the ever-ready preoccupation which can pull the addict out of the doldrums. The cycle then becomes self-perpetuating. Each repetition builds upon the previous experiences and solidifies the reiterative pattern of the addiction. As the cycle fastens its grip on the addict, the addict's life starts to disintegrate and become unmanageable.

Unmanageability

The addict is caught up in the task of keeping his secret life from affecting his "public" life. Even so, the consequences come: arrests, unmasked lies, disruption, unmet commitments, attempts to explain the unexplainable. The addiction surfaces in the addict's inability to manage his or her life. For a moment, the addict recognizes he or she cannot continue. But the impaired mental process blurs reality with euphoric recall of sexual successes. The addict faces yet again the ultimate seduction: a unique opportunity which, of course, will be "the last time."

This unending struggle to manage two lives—"normal" and addictive—continues. The unmanageability takes its toll. Family and friendships are abbreviated and sacrificed. Hobbies are neglected. Finances are affected. Physical needs of other kinds are unattended. The addict's lifestyle becomes a consistent violation of his or her own values, compounding the shame. The impaired mental processes result in faulty problem-solving in all areas of the addict's life. These decisions add to further unmanageability.

Nowhere is this more clear than in the workplace. Faulty problem-solving and diversion of energy require extra time and effort to hold down the job. Extra long hours at work further the unmanageability at home. Worse, if the addiction is connected with the work environment, the addict's position is even more precarious.

Addicts often point to the connection between their addiction and the stress of high performance demands where there is important personal investment. Graduate school, for example, is often when addicts first encounter compulsiveness. The stress of proving one's self in an arena where every inadequacy is evaluated is a potent flashpoint for the ignition of sexual addiction. So are new jobs, promotions, and solo business ventures. Unstructured time, a heavy responsibility for self-direction, and high demands for excellence seem to be the common elements in these situations which are easy triggers for addictive behaviors. Procrastination becomes a daily nemesis for these addicts. For once ignited, the addiction makes work easy to put off.

One of the worst consequences of the addiction is the addicts' *isolation*. The intensity of the double life relates directly to the distance of the addicts from their friends and family. That is, the more intensely involved in compulsive sexual life the addicts become, the more alienated they become from their parents, spouses, and children. Without those human connections, the addicts paradoxically lose touch with their own selves. The unmanageability from the addiction has run its course when there is no longer a double life. When there are no longer friends or family to protect or job to hold or pretenses to be made—even though some things are valued enough to want to stop—the addiction is at its most destructive and violent point. The addict's world has become totally insulated from real life.

The Addictive System

As addicts move from healthy relationships to sexual compulsion, their internal processes combine to form an addictive system. The addictive system—as with all systems—contains subsystems which support one another. Often this support occurs in repetitive, predictable cycles.

To picture the addictive system with its subsystems consider the human body. It is a complex system with many subsystems—the nervous system, digestive system, etc. Clearly, when one subsystem, such as the nervous system, is upset, all the other bodily systems are affected and must adjust in some way.

The addictive system starts with a belief system containing faulty assumptions, myths, and values which support impaired thinking. The resulting delusional thought processes insulate the addiction cycle from reality. The four-phase addiction cycle (preoccupation, ritualization, sexual compulsiveness, and despair) can repeat itself unhindered and take over the addict's life. All the other support systems including relationships, work, finances, and health become unmanageable. The negative consequences from the unmanageability confirm the faulty beliefs which hold that the addict is a bad person who in unlovable. In turn, revalidated beliefs allow further distortion of reality. Diagrammed, the addictive systems looks like this:

THE ADDICTIVE SYSTEM

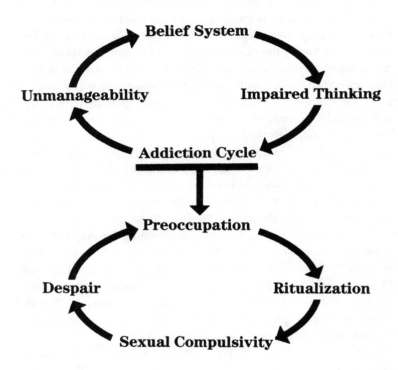

Within the addictive system, *sexual experience becomes the reason for being—the primary relationship for the addict.* For the addict, the sexual experience is the source of nurturing, focus of energy, and origin of excitement. It is the remedy for pain and anxiety, the reward for success, and the means for maintaining emotional balance. Outsiders, especially those who care about the addict, witness the unmanageability and maybe even the behavior. They see the addict's personal loss, the self-degradation, and the abandoned hope and values. It would seem so simple to just stop—even for a while. For the exhibitionist, for example, who may spend up to seven hours a day cruising and another four thinking about it, the task is not so easy. The addiction is truly an altered state of consciousness in which "normal" sexual behavior pales by comparison in terms of excitement and relief from troubles.

In the addict's world, there is an on-going tension between a person's normal self and the addicted self. A Jekyll/Hyde struggle emerges. The addictive system is so compelling that to stop would be like death. Yet, as the system continues, the person's values, priorities, and loved ones are attacked. Sometimes, only a major crisis can restore perspective. Such was the case of Carrie.

Carrie was a music teacher. She was known for boundless energy and creativity in music. She served four elementary schools, carrying heavy equipment from school to school in her old red Volkswagen bus. The kids loved her and she loved them. Colleagues admired her skills. Parents were grateful and attended her concerts in masses.

Carrie had another life as well. Her singing was true and compelling. She received regular engagements at local night spots. She dreamed of being a star. Her singing career, however, never got beyond the local piano bar circuit. No matter how hard she tried, her professional singing career was stymied. As she approached the age of thirty, her disappointment grew into panic that her dream might not happen.

Carrie's sexual addiction started to flourish at the point when she began panicking about her career. In the beginning there were occasional one night stands with hotel customers in bars in which she sang. Then it became every night she worked. The ritual started with her looking over the patrons, selecting the most interesting. Animated conversations during the breaks followed. After finishing, she would go to his room and have sex. Leaving at three or four in the morning, she would return home for a few hours of sleep before school started.

She did not like what she was doing. In the morning, looking at the trusting faces of the children, she would feel the profound incongruity of where she had been but a few hours before. Also, her teaching was slipping as the addiction progressed, though no one really noticed but her. The children were still excited and everyone she worked with was convinced she was great. Still, she knew. She even discovered that being at four different schools made it easier for her to cover when she overslept. She had simply "stopped at one of the other schools."

Carrie also had ceased dating and started singing on weekends. Since she lived alone, her only human contacts were the children and her piano bar customers. What she really wanted was a husband and a family. As her addiction progressed, she began to believe no man would want to be with her if he knew about her life.

The consequence which brought Carrie help was an unexpected heart attack at the age of thirty-three. The short nights had taken their toll. Finally, sitting in a hospital bed, Carrie told her story to a woman chaplain. Amidst deep sobs, she talked of her loneliness and her love of the children. Through her conversations with the chaplain, Carrie acknowledged that the number of men she had slept with in the three-year period was in the hundreds. It was a miracle she had not contracted venereal disease or been injured. The damage to her self-image was penetrating enough.

Carrie, like all sexual addicts, lived in two worlds. One was a world of piano bars, musty hotel rooms, and nameless faces. The other had music, laughter, and faces of children and colleagues—whose names she knew. The co-existence of the two worlds continued until Carrie's body refused to live up to the strain.

Other Addictions and Emotional Illness

One other aspect of the addictive system is that the belief system and delusional thought patterns may support more than one addiction. Overeating, for example, is a way to minimize pain. The sexual addicts who become overweight add shame concerning their body image to their repertoire of pain. The two addictions start to reinforce each other. When the addicts believe that people are not attracted to them, their sexual addiction is partially rooted in the fear of rejection. Then they eat compulsively to kill the pain due to the fear of rejection, and as a result put on weight. The added weight, by their standards, makes them even less desirable. Also, one way to avoid the depression after sexually bingeing is to binge again—with food. The two processes become interdependent. Addicts who have both addictions report that at the height of their sexual addiction, they had their greatest weight problem.

All types of compulsive behavior may be woven into the scenario of sexual addiction.[2] Shoplifting, gambling, spending are frequent counterparts. Physical violence as a way to release pent-up tension is often reported as a concurrent behavior by sexually abusive families. The workaholic who gets high on the excitement of a new deal or a new breakthrough finds professional life even more exhilarating when coupled with the sexual addiction. In that case, the sexual/work addict marries the job.

By far the most common combination of addictions is when the sexual addict is also dependent on alcohol or another drug. Many people attribute sexual excesses and even incest to the power of alcoholism. *The reality is that alcoholism often is a concurrent illness with, rather than the cause of, the sexual addiction.* Many alcoholics have discovered that the treatment of one addiction does not cure the other. There is a growing documentation about the interaction between the two addictions.[3] It may be that one of the greatest, unacknowledged contributors to recidivism in alcoholism is the failure of treatment programs to treat multiple addictions.

Emotional illness flourishes within the addict's world. Depression, suicide, obsessive-compulsiveness, and paranoia are companions to the addiction. Many addicts have received treatment for these mental illnesses while the concomitant sexual addiction is ignored. Yet, the sexual addiction compounded the mental health issues. By far the most devastating emotional risk is suicide.[4] To preserve his integrity, Dr. Jekyll had to kill Mr. Hyde. Some sexual addicts become so desperate during the fourth phase of the addiction cycle (the despair after the compulsive behavior) that the only way out of the double life they can see is to die. Like Dr. Jekyll, sexual addicts' suicidal and depressed feelings express the powerlessness and impotence of living in the addicts' world.

Recovery

Recovery from addiction is the reversal of the alienation that is integral to the addiction. Addicts must establish roots in a caring community. With that support, addicts can stay straight as they struggle for a perspective on their lives. With help, addicts can integrate new beliefs and discard dysfunctional thinking. Without the mood-altering insanity to insulate them from knowledge about their own selves, they become participants in the restoration of their own sanity.

All forms of addiction are vicious because they further the inability to trust others. Yet without help from others, the addict cannot regain control because the addiction feeds itself. The sexual addiction is especially virulent because few forms of fixation or excitement are as super-charged with social judgment, ridicule, or fear. Consequently, seeking help is especially difficult for the sexual addict.

One of the best proven paths to recovery is the Twelve Steps of Alcoholics Anonymous.[5] Many people suffering from compulsive disorders have translated the Steps for their own use such as Overeaters Anonymous, Gamblers Anonymous, and Emotions Anonymous. This book proposes the Twelve Steps as a way for sexual addicts to emerge from their double lives. Across the country local groups have modified the Twelve Steps for the sexually compulsive.

The Twelve Step Program helps members restore the living network of human relationships—especially in the family. The Program asks the addicts first to accept their addiction by looking at their addiction cycle and its consequences, i.e., to admit that they are powerless over their sexual behavior and their lives have become unmanageable. With that admission, the members then are able to start the rebuilding of relationships by taking responsibility for what they have done and making amends where possible. Values and priorities are reclaimed. Throughout the Program, members explore basic spiritual issues as a way of understanding and facing their anxiety. As members live the Program, the double life with all its delusion and pain can be left behind. Chapter six of this book describes in detail how the Twelve Steps can help the sexual addict break out of the addicts' world.

This chapter has described the cycle of the sexual addiction. Before proceeding further, we must survey the many forms sexual addiction can take. No assessment of the sexual addiction would be complete without showing its potential variations. The question to be answered is who are the inhabitants of the addicts' world. That is the task of the next chapter.

2

The Levels of Addiction

Herb, 34, is a traveling salesman who maintains an apartment in Minneapolis for his regular visits to the city. He is married and has two children. He says he earns about $35,000 a year. Herb says he has a good relationship with his wife of seven years, but that spending nearly half of his life on the road drives him to prostitutes.

At the same time, he admits that he probably would continue to visit prostitutes—although not as frequently—even if his work did not keep him away from home so much.

Herb said he has been patronizing prostitutes for nine years and seeks encounters on an average of two or three times a week when he is not at home.

"I think of them as therapy," Herb said, "and I'm serious now. I usually go during the middle of the day, and it's often when something's bugging me. I've had a bad morning or a sale has gone sour.

"Instead of going out to lunch and downing two or three martinis, I like to have a woman."

Minneapolis Star
October 7, 1976.

We live in a time where the "joy of sex" is seen as the rightful pursuit of everyone. To be celibate, in fact, is almost to be suspect. As part of the sexual revolution, inhibitions and hang-ups are to be discarded. In many ways, this shift in our cultural mores constitutes a breakthrough in the exploration of human sexuality. It is an important antidote to the proscriptive past and a significant acknowledgment of our sexual nature. As in all major culture changes, there are excesses. Our preoccupation with sex pervades almost all facets of our contemporary life-styles. In an age which highly values the variety and quality of sexual experience, there is a group which is overlooked: those who are sexually compulsive in ways they do not want to be.

To view sexual addicts as people who are simply guilt-ridden because of sexual behavior is to completely misunderstand the nature of the addiction. This viewpoint assumes that addicts need to be more free and enjoy sexuality and that they feel bad because of unhelpful scruples and misinformation. An example is masturbation, which is now generally accepted as a developmental phase and a natural expression of personal sexuality. For the man who masturbates so often that he has at times severly injured his penis, it is no longer just a question of accepting his desire to masturbate. His masturbation is seriously affecting his life and bringing harmful consequences to his body.

Sexual addicts feel the pain and consequences. They recognize the personal emptiness. If they are lucky, they may have some sense of the exploitation and harm to others. They wrestle daily with the fear of discovery of their compulsivity. This is not to suggest that sexual addicts are uninhibited and free of hang-ups. On the contrary, they often do come from highly proscriptive families and carry damaging myths inside them. Part of recovery always is restructuring the belief system by acquiring adequate information and accepting one's own sexuality. The first task of recovery, however, is to focus on the uncontrollable behavior.

When discussing sexual addiction, it is necessary to recognize that not everyone who has a regrettable sexual experience is an addict. There are people who have regrets over specific events, realizing that their sexual behavior on a given occasion was not in their best interest. They add it to their experience and simply do not repeat it. There are numbers who have abused their sexuality. Going on a sexual binge, for example, might occur after a graduation or in retaliation to a lover's indiscretion.

There are also those who have episodes of compulsivity. Those who study middle-age transition, the famous "middle-scence," note the sexual bingeing which can occur at that time. Also, it is often seen as a post-divorce pattern. The divorced person, who is suddenly free from marital obligations, may experiment to excess. Adolescents struggle with the intensity of their emerging sexuality. Adolescent sexual expression is a key conflict area between peer support and parental proscription. Experimentation and exploration are part of identity formation. Learning from youthful enthusiasm is part of internalizing appropriate rules and boundaries. In that sense, adolescence does parallel the "middlescence" search for self. Thus, episodes of sexual excess may only indicate changing life circumstances. [1]

Also, there are those who may have a problem, but not necessarily an addiction. Consider the story of Don, a college professor nationally recognized for his careful scholarship. On occasion he had the urge to go to a porno theater. While watching the movie, he would masturbate, which he found very exciting. When leaving, however, an immense depression would always come over him. He felt degraded. He worried about being recognized—or worse—arrested. He would always vow not to repeat the experience. Over a period of eight years, he had done it four to five times.

Don's problem has some important parallels with sexual addiction. The excitement/depression scenario is a common story for the addict. So are breaking the rules and the excitement of the illicit. Also, the vow to quit or make it the last time is part and parcel of the addiction. Yet, Don is not an addict. This is not to minimize his problem which is painful and abusive. He runs the risk of adverse consequences, but, in general, his life has not become unmanageable. In short, he has not entered the addict's world. Were Don to experience periods in which he repeated the behavior frequently with damaging results he clearly would have an addictive pattern. Many addicts describe their experiences as episodic—that is, periodic binges—which have several consequences to their work, relationships, and self-esteem. Between binges, they may experience extended periods with no problems. Being able to stop for a period of time provides the illusion of control, which makes it more difficult for the addict to acknowledge that there is a problem. As years pass, however, a pattern of bingeing reveals an unmistakable addiction. For some addicts, the bingeing becomes so frequent, the behavior is almost constant.

If Don's situation were changed again and his visits to the theater were a part of a much larger picture, including massage parlors, strip shows, and multiple affairs, his actions also would have a very different meaning. A clear case of addiction can emerge when other forms of sexual compulsiveness are considered as well. The assessment of the addiction's extent or intensity is complete only with first examining the varieties of sexual addiction.

Levels of Addiction

Addicts often comment in group therapy that they are astounded at how similar their experiences were, even though what they did was vastly different. While the varieties of addiction are great, the sexual addiction cycle described in chapter one is common. Categorizing the various forms of sexual compulsiveness into different groups, however, helps in a number of ways. First, grouping provides perspective of the wide range of sexual behaviors in which addiction can thrive. From this perspective addicts can make a better inventory of the scope of their addiction. Second, some sexual behavior involves great danger, breaks the law, or victimizes others. For the addicts, these behaviors show greater powerlessness and unmanageability. To risk greater consequences in the interest of a more exciting high indicates the *escalation of the addiction*. Finally, every addict must understand his or her own unique pattern of sexually compulsive behavior. Subtle differences are extremely important for addicts, especially in early recovery. For example, strategies for avoiding unique cues and rituals which initiate the addictive cycle can be developed once a pattern is identified. To interrupt the addictive cycle the addict must understand his or her pattern of behavior. Creating a framework for the behavior has made that task easier.

A workable structure which helps to identify patterns is to view the addiction as operating at three levels. The first level, Level One, contains behaviors which are regarded as normal, acceptable, or tolerable. Examples include masturbation, homosexuality, and prostitution. Level Two, by contrast, extends to those behaviors which are clearly victimizing and for which legal sanctions are enforced. These are generally seen as nuisance offenses such as exhibitionism or voyeurism. The Level Three behaviors have grave consequences for the victims and legal consequences for the addicts such as incest, child molestation, or rape. Compulsivity at this level represents a severe progression of the addiction.

Suggesting three levels does not mean that addicts cannot destroy their lives with Level One behavior. Many addicts have done just that without ever venturing into Levels Two or Three. It would be unusual, however, for an addict to be compulsive at Levels Two or Three without a significant amount of compulsivity at Level One. Most rare is the addict who simply focuses on only one form of sexual compulsiveness. But that, too, does happen. Within a level or across levels, the addict must understand the full range of possibilities.

Level One

Level One behaviors have in common general cultural acceptance. If some are regarded as unseemly or even illegal, the reality is that widespread practice conveys a public tolerance. The other common characteristic is that each can be devastating when done compulsively. Even the healthiest forms of human sexual expression can turn into self-defeating behaviors—or worse—the victimization of the others.

Masturbation

Masturbation is an essential part of being a sexual person. Nurturing oneself, exploring sexual needs and fantasies, and establishing a basic self-knowledge are vital contributions that masturbation makes to sexual identity. As sexual therapists are keenly aware, without these factors it is more difficult to have a vital sexual relationship. In fact, for people who suffer from sexual dysfunction, therapy often involves a careful rebuilding of a patient's attitudes and beliefs around masturbation.

For the addict, however, masturbation becomes a degrading event. Masturbating four to five times a day for years on end becomes a secret life. It is the central part of every day. At the least feeling of frustration or loneliness, the addict struggles to find a private place to masturbate. Unlocking the office door, walking out of the bathroom, or driving in the car, the addict is certain that no one else is as obsessed as he is.

Part of that certainty comes from the collection of judgments and beliefs he holds to be true about masturbation. Messages from parents, family, and church have left no doubt that it is a character flaw. As a result, the addict may carry some equation in his or her head: masturbation equals failure. Masturbation equals a loss of manhood. Masturbation is not feminine. Masturbation equals punishment.

One addict tells a story about his Catholic upbringing. Each Saturday, his father would ask if the boy had to go to confession. Since masturbation was a sin, both boy and father knew what had to be confessed. The father would talk to the boy about how he would become a man when he conquered his urges. The boy would sit in his shame. He dreaded Saturdays.

It later turned out that the father was simply telling his own belief—his own myth to the boy. The father was a compulsive masturbator who believed that his problem was simply lack of self-control. In his desperation to prevent the same pain for his son, the father relayed the myth which locked him into his own addiction. (The same image of ideal manliness which added to the father's shame was passed on to his son.) Paradoxically, he re-created the same addictive system for his son out of love. As addicts go, this is a common story.

The son translated the message in a particularly damaging way. He felt that God would punish him for his masturbation. In fact, he believed that nothing would go right for him for the twenty-four hours following each time he masturbated. Given the power of his expectations and his daily masturbation, his life was an unending cycle of failure and disappointments. His compulsive masturbating was central to the self-fulfilling prophecy of God's punishment.

Heterosexual Relationships

Addiction can manifest itself in a heterosexual relationship in a number of ways. At the most elementary level, addiction is present when one partner sacrifices important parts of the total relationship in the service of sexual needs. A warning sign is when a spouse or signifcant other starts to feel victimized by the other's sexuality. (The warning intensifies when exploited feelings are dismissed.) Discounting the spouse's feelings trades relationship needs for sexual needs. Every relationship has times when sexual needs are not matched. The addict, however, makes the other person an obsession. For the partner, the relationship is contingent on sexual performance. Both partners lose the freedom, fun, and intimacy of mutual loving sexual play. Sexuality ceases to be nurturing, growing, and life-enhancing. Addiction renders a relationship empty, joyless, and demoralizing.

Some addicts seek refuge in multiple relationships. Consider the woman whose loneliness is enhanced by the unending series of one-night stands. Try as she will, she cannot stop the blur of faces and bodies. Or take the man who seldom has one relationship but is "meaningfully" involved with several simultaneously. When he stops to be honest, he may admit not even liking his sexual partners. To have perceived the relationships as meaningful was a delusion used to get into bed. The human dilemma of whether it is possible to love more than one person at once is not what is in question. At issue here is the fear of having to live without sex. Or in addiction terms—the addict must protect the supply.

Cruising is one of the ultimate activities for the desperate addict. Hustling in bars, streets, and parties is characterized by the contrast of excitement and loneliness. Will I be chosen? Will I score? Even the prospect is exhilarating. Memories of successful forays, the smells, the music, the adventures cloak the sadness. The pursuit of sexual excitement extends to professional, business, and educational settings. However, the void that sex attempts to fill remains the same.

Chris, for example, was an addict whose cruising was fused with her professional life as a consultant in urban planning. Her ability to articulate clearly the complex problems of her field plus her charisma and attractiveness made her a speaker in high demand. Her life was filled with seminars, conferences, and workshops. They served as a cover for her other life. Her traveling maximized her sexual opportunities. She had on-going relationships in each of the cities she visited regularly. One-night stands were even more common. With hindsight, she was later to say that to travel was to be sexual. It started as soon as she stepped on the plane. Her career was a potent catalyst to the addiction.

Cruising as a search for sexual excitement can even occur within the context of marriage—sometimes with tragic results. Fred and Liza were considered the ideal couple by their friends. Sweethearts at fourteen and married at twenty, their addiction problems started when both were in graduate school. Liza had come home one night after being at a bar and confessed to Fred that she had been picked up and "made." Fred's response was unexpected. He found it exciting and made ardent love to her. He asked her to do it again with similar results. Soon their lovemaking became a ritual in which Liza would seduce a man, report all the details to Fred, and make love with Fred.

As the excitement became old, Fred encouraged Liza to bring the men home. Fred would masturbate as he watched the men with his wife. Eventually, he took more of an active role in orchestrating the activities—which became progressively more degrading to Liza. After years, their married life was organized around these events. When they finally sought therapy, the striking part of their story was how each had longed to stop. They had even made mutual efforts to stop—especially one time when Liza was injured. The central part of their recovery was in reclaiming their very real love of one another.

Centerfolds, Pornography, and Strip Shows

Playboy, Oui, Penthouse, Hustler, and other magazines are available at drugstores, grocery stores, and even the neighborhood "Quickstop." There are R-rated movies and X-rated movies. Porno shops abound. Erotic art has been legitimized. The human body is a career focus for some of the best photographers. Many establishments feature topless and bottomless entertainment to bring in patrons. The more refined use "lingerie" shows. The advent of videotape and cable TV has added many new dimensions to hotel rooms, porno shops, and even the bedroom. Nude beaches are no longer uncommon.

Some of the sexual art is creative, some is erotic, some reflects shifts in cultural boundaries. Some is titillating. Some is crass commercialism. Some is realism. Some is boring. Some is in bad taste.

Taken together, a veritable smorgasbord of obsession for the addict exists. One common element is the excitement. The other is the sexual object. The addict can transform even the most refined forms of human nudity into his own particular fusion of loneliness and arousal. The absence of a relationship and the desire for heightened excitement are the twin pillars of the sexual addiction. Nowhere is this more clear than when the addiction is visual.

Visual addiction does not always have obvious consequences. It is common to see men straining their necks as they drive to watch an attractive woman walk down a street on a summer day. The addict, however, will turn around to go by her a second time—perhaps nearly causing an accident—in an effort to watch her again. Endless hours go by browsing in a porno bookstore, sitting in the beach parking lot, driving around a college campus, tennis courts, and shopping malls, a nightly habit of stopping at the topless bar. Soon the time takes its toll. Work does not get done and excuses are made. Lies are told to the family about the long work hours.

Money starts to be a problem. For instance, money needed for family expenses is spent on pornography and sexually explicit magazines or an expensive videotape machine used for porno films. Then there is the camera equipment for a hobby not enjoyed, except for the excitement of asking people to pose.

The worst is that after a time, the obsession becomes more

important than being in an important relationship. The watching becomes a high more important than family and friends. But, rationalizes the addict, there is no harm in watching.

Prostitution

Every now and then a vice squad will close in on an outcall service which has made prostitutes available to customers by phone. Records are seized. A chill goes through the city. Eight to ten thousand men wonder if their names were kept on file. The paper accentuates this fear by printing the police comment that the list of patrons included prominent government officials, religious leaders, and businessmen. Each patron, in his shame, fears that his name has surfaced. All rehearse confessions and stories for their bosses and wives. The public feels sensation and fear, glimpsing for a moment the large network of people who make prostitution a part of their lives.

Prostitution appears in many forms. Some outcall services are so large they have representatives in the major metropolitan areas of the country. Simply call a toll-free number. Massage, rap, and sauna parlors will charge their services on major credit cards. Many metropolitan hotels are routinely worked by young, often beautiful women. Businesses hire public relations "consultants." Listening to a CB radio one quickly becomes aware of vans and pickups driven by women with handles like "Bunny" or "Snuggles." They work the nation's truck stops and rest areas. These forms of the "oldest profession" do not generate public reaction.

Somehow concern is generated only for the streetwalker who works the bars and streets under the tyranny of a pimp. Or the adolescent runaway who ends up a prostitute to survive. Or the young boy who works as a "chicken" in gay cruising areas. The issue of whether prostitution is a victimless crime goes beyond the scope of this book. Our focus of concern is on the addict whose involvement with prostitution is crippling his or her life.

Addicts who use the Twelve Steps will often joke about going to "Johns Anonymous" because of the prevalence of prostitution in the sexual addiction and the usage by prostitutes of the word "John" to describe their customers. Addicts like prostitutes because it is an immediate fix with few entanglements. Often it is anonymous. Yet, the consequences of prostitution are high. The lies often are elaborate. There is risk of disease. There is the possibility of it becoming public knowledge. Yet, the biggest factor for most addicts is the expense. A habit of three to four visits a week is expensive to sustain. One addict, a physician, used up all the equity from the sale of an expensive home in prostitution.

For family men even more lies are required to explain where the money has gone. When addicts tell about themselves, their stories are frequently punctuated with deep sobs as they tell of the times when they would come home after spending a hundred dollars on a prostitute, only to realize that their children and wives were doing without something they needed. However, as in all addiction, painful realization does not stop compulsive behavior.

Our understanding of prostitutes needs to be expanded. We are aware of women who sell their services because of financial desperation or a drug habit. We also know the impact of sexual and physical abuse from which prostitutes recycle the dramas of their own early family experiences. We know about runaways and pimps. We have even heard of happy hookers. Less aware are we of the woman addict who buries her pain with sexual obsession. Prostitution, even part-time, can be a way to get paid for a compulsive sexual need. For some prostitutes who fail to understand this part of themselves, it is very difficult to stop.

Homosexuality

Recent decades have witnessed the struggle of homosexual people to establish themselves in the eyes of the straight community. Despite increased acceptance, there remains in our culture shame and judgment of what is seen as "perverse." Our lack of knowledge is underlined by increasing efforts to understand the origins of homosexuality.

For gay or lesbian persons who are also sexual addicts, compulsivity simply compounds problems of acceptance and shame. For the sexual addict whose self-image is already marginal, adding the problems of sexual identity intensifies all sexual issues. The gay man who has eight to ten sexual encounters with different partners during a week's time has little chance to develop a real sense of self because of his loneliness and isolation. If those encounters are under degrading or even dangerous circumstances, self-image suffers further.

Jim was a Lutheran seminarian. He went to school full-time and worked part-time as a youth director in a parish. He was sensitive, intelligent, and committed to his career. He was also driven by his sexual compulsion. His pattern was to frequent at night a well-known park area by a local river which was known as a gay "cruising" area. He would stand by the same tree each time and allow himself to be picked up. His sexual contacts were in the dark with strangers. He always felt humiliated. One time he was severely beaten.

What prompted Jim to seek help was not a "river" incident. Rather, he was sexual with one of the young adults in the parish he served who had visited him at his apartment. He became aware of how vulnerable he was and in his fear sought therapy. Once in therapy, he realized he really had two issues. First, his homosexual orientation would be a problem in his ministry. And second, his sexual compulsiveness was an obstacle to developing significant relationships. His issues around homosexuality were compounded by his sexual addiction.

The addiction is even more complicated for men who consider themselves heterosexual, but are compulsive only in homosexual ways. Steve, for example, saw himself as happily married. During a particularly stressful period, he got involved with a man in a restroom in his office building. He repeated the experience a couple of days later. Within a few months, he was a regular in the "hot johns" in his area. In time he expanded into porno shops, meeting men in the movie booths. This lasted for a period of four years.

Two events brought Steve to therapy. The first was that he met his brother walking through the booths at the porno store. He immediately acknowledged to himself that his brother was as troubled as he. Second, while traveling he had sex with a man in a service station toilet while his wife and kids waited in the car. During therapy Steve realized that seeing his brother recalled all those heavily weighted family messages he carried about sexuality and homosexuality. Finally, he had to recognize that his family life was not happy. Comfortable, but not intimate. The service station episode simply underscored that he was lonely in the midst of those he loved.

The Level One Addict

Level One addicts seldom stay with one behavior category. More common would be an addict for whom prostitution, affairs, visits to porno shops, and occasional visits to hot johns form an overall picture of obsession. The accumulated effect is that the addiction can become the center of the addict's life—rooted in a complex malaise of deceit, isolation, and shame.

Many Level One addicts believe they can control their behavior since it is not constant. They experience episodes in which they simply sexually binge. Then they stop for weeks or even months. A salesman, for example, may only use prostitutes when he travels. In town, he perceives his life as "normal." Vows to quit made upon return from his last trip are forgotten with the next. Because of the appearance of "normalcy," he rationalizes that he can handle his behavior and that it has no impact on his life. Yet, he truly has a secret world where damaging consequences subtly overtake him. Normal persons do not carry the secrets and shame he does. He does not stop because he cannot.

The problem for the Level One addicts is that they can rationalize that they are not much different from most folks. While they feel unique in desperateness and obsession, the sexual behavior creates few real social consequences. Yet the addicts pay a personal toll in increasing pain and loneliness. The next level of addiction, however, involves clear violations of cultural norms—and therefore, greater risk. Also, greater excitement.

Level Two

Level Two addictive behaviors are sufficiently intrusive to warrant stiff legal sanctions. Exhibitionism, voyeurism, indecent phone calls, and indecent liberties all are punished when actively prosecuted. Both prosecutors and the general public, however, view these acts as nuisance offenses. The offenders are seen as pathetic and usually unable to establish effective relationships.[2] Yet, there are victims and there are sanctions. The consequences and danger are clearly part of the addictive process. Common to all Level Two obsessions is that someone is victimized.

Exhibitionism

Gene Abel of the New York State Psychiatric Institute reports exhibitionist clients who have exposed themselves two to three hundred times with few or no arrests.[3] There is consensus about the reasons. Fear of reporting, indifference, and cynicism about impact are a few. One of the biggest reasons is that victims seldom get accurate descriptions. The result is that an addict's actions can go unchecked quite some time. Therefore, what starts as some experimentation can quickly become a flourishing addiction with little interference.

Stereotypically, a flasher is a person who wears a raincoat on sunny days. However, the truth is that exhibitionists are remarkably diverse in their methods, such as:

- Driving or parking in a car with pants pulled down.
- Leaving the pants' zipper open and standing in an elevator, on a street, or in a phone booth.
- Having a "strategic" hole in a pair of jeans or shorts.
- Wearing swimming trunks without liners.
- Leaving curtains "inadvertently" ajar in bedroom or bathroom.
- Ringing a doorbell in a secluded doorway and exposing when it is answered.
- Walking exposed in shopping malls, campuses, open areas.
- Approaching a building with large windows such as a library or an apartment building and exposing through the window.

Actually, there are many people who witness an act of exposing who are either unaware of the exhibitionist's intention or dismiss their own judgment as "paranoia." To expose without raising alarm becomes part of the challenge for the exhibitionist. It also limits the consequences of the addiction.

The method involving the highest risk for the exposer is the use of an automobile. Victims often have sufficient presence of mind to get a license number. Yet, driving is a very common practice. The addict can escape quickly in a car if necessary and cover more ground in search of women. Exhibitionists who drive while exposing almost invariably report car accidents as one of the consequences of their addiction. They are totally entranced by their approach to their victim and simply do not watch where they are going.

For the exhibitionist whose pattern involves driving, simply entering a car becomes a cue to start the ritual. Scanning streets for potential "scores" becomes almost part of driving. Certain streets and areas become routes which are regularly checked. The addict cannot trust that he will arrive at his intended destination, because driving itself has become a real part of the ritual. Some addicts count making it to work on time a major victory, for once an addict begins cruising, three to six hours may go by before he stops.

The human cost is incredible. Exhibitionists lead double lives. They live with the constant fear that someone who has seen them in their street roles will recognize them in their "other" lives. Worse, they judge themselves by the same standards society uses—as weird, nuisance perverts. That judgment is not accurate since there is trauma for the victim. Being accosted by an exposer can be very damaging and frightening. Even most exhibitionists carry an image of a person's face whom they know they have hurt. Both society and the addict underestimate the danger and the cost of the addiction.

Voyeurism

"Peeping Toms," like flashers, have their stereotypes. The ineffectual bachelor peering into the neighboring apartment via the telescope may seem harmless. For voyeur addicts, however, peeping is usually not their only compulsive behavior. Quite often, they become involved in other addictive behaviors such as pornography, movies, and strip shows. Moreover, being quite inventive in voyeurism is characteristic. Addicts have many stories about heat vents, mirrors, and cameras. Some of their efforts involve great risk, including peering into house or apartment windows—or even hiding in closets.

Over and above the obvious costs—including risk of arrest, most voyeurs agree one of the biggest losses is time. Watching a window for three or four hours—often under very awkward circumstances—in the hope of glimpsing ninety seconds of nudity is insane even to the addict. Voyeurs report that while waiting, they often struggle with themselves asking, "Why am I doing this?" They make a commitment to stop waiting by a certain time if nothing happens. Yet, the time comes and goes. They sit and continue to wait—until either something does happen or it is obvious nothing will. Each episode is followed by depression and pain. The loss of time and energy, the deep embarrassment about being a voyeur, the self-hatred at being unable to control oneself combine to keep an addict absolutely isolated. There is one simple way to alleviate the pain temporarily. Do it again.

As with most addicts, the voyeur is sustained by excitement. He waits in a trance-like state, with energies focused in the waiting. Totally absorbed, the addict loses all contact with reality, save for focus of the addiction. Cares, worries, deadlines, and responsibilities are for a blessed moment, suspended. The mood-altering qualities of the experience are enhanced by the intrusive, the stolen, the illicit parts of the behavior. Objectively, the voyeur could go to the local topless bar and see more with less risk and discomfort. He could have sex with someone who wants to have sex with him. Or he could pay for sex. But it is not the same.

The excitement of illicit victimization is rooted in the addicts' anger. Breaking the rules is a way to retaliate for hurts, real and imagined. The anger stems from a set of beliefs, family messages, and self-judgments the addicts use to interpret the world. Most addicts do not connect their behavior with anger. The excitement and arousal of the trance block the feelings, along with the rest of the pain.

The greater the anger and pain, the more excitment required to block it. This dynamic is the key to understanding how escalation occurs within the addictive process. If the current behavior within the addictive cycle is no longer supplying the excitement necessary to block the pain, something with greater risk is attempted. A good example is the addict who is a combination voyeur-exhibitionist.

The Voyeur-Exhibitionist

Voyeurism and exhibitionism often go together. The connecting link is masturbation. For the voyeur, masturbating while watching is another way of enhancing the excitement.

The addict finds a position in which he can watch attractive women walk by, but in which he cannot be seen. This is usually a car, a first-floor restroom, office, or bedroom, or even a portable outhouse of the type found in beaches, parks, and rest areas. The thrill is in ejaculating within a few feet of a woman without her knowledge. Masturbating in front of her is but a fragile step away.

Pete is an addict who took that step. His sexual history from the seventh grade on was characterized by compulsive masturbation and involvement with many girls or women at the same time. He met a woman, Angie, with whom he fell in love in his junior year of college. They were married shortly after his graduation.

Pete landed a job as a salesman for a large grain firm. Because of his potential as a businessman, he was given a huge territory with very little guidance as to how to manage it. Accountability was high, but only on a semi-annual basis. The result was Pete had a lot of unstructured time and very little support. He was totally overwhelmed.

Although he had only been married a little while, he was already feeling restless. His sexual relationship with Angie was excellent, yet he missed his "woman-chasing." Late one night, he went for a walk. Noting an open window, he found himself watching a neighborhood teenager undress. It was the greatest sexual arousal he could remember. This event initiated a year of intense voyeurism all over the city.

Pete had an extraordinary gift of gab, and people trusted him. Nonetheless, his charm could not cover that he was not doing his job. His boss transferred him to a less demanding territory, but equally unstructured. Pete felt demoralized. He saw himself as a procrastinator. He also blamed his peeping, which was taking a lot of his energy. He was committed to proving himself in his job, but repeated efforts to stop his voyeurism failed.

Pete's sexual demands on his wife were increasing and becoming more insensitive. Angie was starting to complain about being pestered. Angie and Pete also had a baby, so that Angie's energy was absorbed in child care. Pete felt abandoned at a time when he was now the sole financial support of the family.

One summer night, Pete had parked near a college campus. He was watching the windows of the women's dorm. He also enjoyed watching and listening as the young women walked past his car. He started masturbating in the car. It was exhilarating. He soon started driving around at night masturbating and exposing. In a short time he tried it in the daytime. To his surprise, some would watch and some would avert their eyes. Nothing else happened.

Within a few weeks, Pete's life was almost totally involved in exposing himself. He would start for work and he would make it if there were meetings he had to attend. Otherwise, he would end up cruising in his car. He began to know the city in a different way—the rhythm of the city in terms of when and where women would be: colleges in the morning, shopping malls at noon, parks and schools in the afternoon. Sometimes he would voyeur at night.

Usually when he came home, he was exhausted. Sometimes he would go to bed without supper. Angie thought he was overworking. The reality was his trance-like search coupled with masturbating for hours left him drained.

Like all addicts, Pete became entangled in a complex web—lies and deceits with his boss, as well as his wife. He had to explain his absences and failures to perform. What was worse was that he had broken his own rule and was becoming involved with a secretary at work. He also visited his first prostitute. He was woman-chasing again.

There were times at the end of an all-day binge when he felt his life was out of control. He would break down sobbing over his steering wheel. He vowed to stop each time. But he would resume, maybe even that night. He often thought of himself as being like a heroin addict.

One spring day he had the peak exhibitionist experience. A young woman had put her head in the window of the car, talked to him, and watched him maturbate to ejaculation. He was still in that transitory mood of elation and peacefulness as he pulled into the driveway. There a squad car was waiting. Angie was on the back steps holding the baby, looking absolutely terrified. The image was burned on his soul, for in one moment the consequences of his addiction were placed in sharp relief against everything he cherished and loved.

Pete got help because of thoughtful police intervention, but not before he lost his job which happened a few days later. His termination was not related to his arrest, but obviously was connected to his addiction. Usually a fullblown addiction occurs over a long period of time, but Pete's story illustrates how the sexual addiction can destroy a person in less than two years.

The escalation of the addiction matches the increasing pain, isolation, and shame. The voyeur-exhibitionist combination is a potent illustration. Another set of Level Two behaviors which share the same process is usually called by society as "indecent."

Indecent Calls and Liberties

Indecent phone calls occur when the addict calls a woman in order to make suggestive statements, to ask intrusive or embarrassing sexual questions, or to assault her verbally. Compared with the voyeur-exhibitionist, the difference is that victimization occurs visually with one and orally with the other. Masturbation serves as an important link here as well. Addicts will start by masturbating while talking on the phone to a woman who is not aware of it. Soon, however, efforts to be more explicit about the sexual intrusion follow.

Indecent liberties are inappropriate touches—sometimes referred to as mini-rapes. Here too addicts follow a path of escalating addiction. In the press of a crowded subway or shopping mall, the brush of a hand against a thigh or breast can be regarded as accidental. In the rush, it is hard not to bump into someone. Addicts tell stories about what they would do to "have accidents" in the company of their spouses or children. Loved ones become a cover—the incongruity of which adds to the addicts' shame. All the ingredients are present: the stolen, the illicit, the exciting.

Escalation with indecent liberties takes a significant departure. Touching others with their knowledge but without their permission is the next step. For a woman to know clearly that she has been fondled against her will creates a level of intrusion that is truly frightening. Society's response to the sexual abuse is that a nuisance has been transformed into a punishable personal violation. The addict knows that fact. To be compulsive to that degree in spite of the obvious consequences is to propel the addict into Level Three of sexual behavior.

Level Three

The common element of Level Three behavior is that some of our most significant boundaries are violated. Rape, incest, and child molesting are basic transgressions of laws designed to protect the vulnerable. There is little compassion or understanding for someone compulsive at this level. Yet, addiction exists here too. Whether or not there *should* be compassion or understanding is another issue. That addiction exists here is a fact.

Child Molesting and Incest

The addict who focuses on children usually has suffered some interruption in his or her own development while growing up. There is a part of the addict which is not any older than the victim. Actual behavior may span all three levels of addiction, including compulsive masturbation with child pornography, child prostitution, voyeuristic and exposing behavior with children, as well as molestation. There are child molesters who are compulsive with adults as well. In those situations, the addict has a preference—either child before adult, or adult before child. Further complicating factors reside in the sexual identity of the addict, i.e., man or woman, homosexual or heterosexual.

The sexual abuse of children has a long history far beyond the scope of this book. As our awareness grows of its extent, the more we know of its damage. Abuse is a major factor in the transmission of sexual compulsivity from one generation to the next. Nowhere is this more evident than in the family where incest takes place.

What a child learns from a parent is how to have a relationship. When a parent is sexual with a child, the child concludes at a fundamental level that in order to have a relationship, one has to be sexual. Thus, all relationships become sexualized. Fathers and mothers are naturally attracted to their children. One of the gifts of parenthood is not to act on those feelings. Those who argue for the right of children to be sexual with their parents miss the developmental point.

Vern was intensely active sexually with his two daughters for an eight-year period. The fact did not come out until his family was brought in during his treatment for alcoholism. He knew his behavior was wrong and had struggled repeatedly to stop. As part of his therapy, Vern had to confront the fact that he had been sexually abused by both his mother and father. When talking with his dad who was still alive, he discovered that the abuse transcended four generations. His father too had been abused. Vern also had to acknowledge that his sexual addiction extended to pornography, many affairs, and extensive involvement with prostitutes.

A situation similar to incest exists for professionals such as physicians or therapists whose patients are like children in their vulnerability. For the professional to be sexual with them also is to betray a trust. The sexual addict who exploits professional client relationships is in reality committing a type of incest.

Remember, however, behavior by itself does not make an addict. Further, to have feelings of attraction for a child (or a client) does not constitute addiction. Even to act on those feelings, as damaging as that would be, does not make an addict. Addicts are people who cannot stop their behavior which is crippling them and those around them.

Rape and Violence

Violent fantasies are common in human beings. These fantasies reflect cultural attitudes which see force and violence as an inevitable part of human sexuality. Feminists have long been outspoken critics of abusive norms in our "sick society." Their criticisms have a solid empirical basis. Neil Malamuth, a psychologist from the University of Manitoba, writes:

> Research we and other investigators have conducted strongly supports the feminist viewpoint. It has been found that within the normal population many men have the type of physiological, attitudinal, and behavioral tendencies paralleling those of rapists. Moreover, the belief system of both males and females clearly shows a pattern that condones the use of force in sexual relationships.[4]

Clearly, rape and violence are the tips of a large cultural iceberg.

If many people have the potential for violence, what is it that brings some to the point of rape? Some argue that rape stems from a fundamental lawlessness. One of the very best surveys of the literature on this subject is *Sex Crime and the Law* by MacNamara and Sagarin, stating:

> Most arrests are of males of low social-economic status, and the fact that such a high percentage of the rapists had also been arrested for property crimes would strongly suggest a ghetto or poverty background and a general orientation of disrespect for the law. More important, they are in the main not people who are psychopathically involved as oversexualized beings or persons with uncontrollable sexual impulses. With few exceptions, they do not seem to be "career rapists," or even "career sex criminals," although they might be seen as career criminals.[5]

While MacNamara and Sagarin describe an important perspective on the overall issue of rape, another way to view rape is to see it as part of a general pattern of compulsivity. Rape can be the most extreme expression of escalation in the sexual addiction. However, not all rapists are addicts, but some addicts are rapists. A good example is the case of George. George was an appliance repairman. He was extremely skillful at figuring out how to make things work again. He took pride in that. He was also proud of his wife, son, and three daughters. The secret in the family was George's alcoholism which everyone shielded from the outside world. The family attributed their problems to his drinking. For the outside world, his craftsmanship and his dependability were well recognized. He was Catholic and served several terms as parish trustee.

George led another life as well—the life of a sexual addict in the advanced stages. About two years before he was married, George had been arrested for exhibitionism. Now at the age of forty-three, he had been arrested again. His secret life was revealed and he was forced into treatment. His therapist required that George complete alcoholism treatment first. Then George started on treatment for his sexual addiction.

George's list of sexual compulsivity was lengthy. Compulsive masturbation usually with pornography, voyeurism, and exhibitionism were weekly and sometimes daily events. He had many affairs, including one with a customer which lasted four years. One of his "secrets" involved his being so trustworthy his customers would leave him alone in the house to do repairwork. He liked to explore dresser drawers and finger underclothing, panties, and bras. Prostitution was a major part of his lifestyle. At one point, he had to obtain a secret loan for $2,700 to cover withdrawals he had made to pay for prostitutes. In the year before his arrest, George had also raped six women at knifepoint. He had physically molested seven others.

George's story is not atypical. Compulsive rapists report the presence of many Level One and Two behaviors as part of their paths. This does not mean that sexual addiction leads inexorably to being a rapist. It does mean that to see prostitution, pornography, exhibitionism, and voyeurism as mere nuisances is to misunderstand the nature of sexual addiction. Some addicts commit rape as part of their overall compulsivity.

Another example is the story of Bill, who was referred by a criminal justice diversion project for his exhibitionism. Shortly after beginning therapy he was referred to a hospital in-patient program for his alcoholism. After treatment, he re-joined his therapy group for dealing with his sexual addiction. He initially maintained that his exhibitionism was limited to driving around masturbating in his car. He eventually admitted to a twelve-year history of exhibitionism. In addition, he told of numerous affairs, in one of which he fathered a child. Prostitution was also a significant part of his history. With the group's assistance he was able to calculate that he had spent in excess of $10,000 on prostitutes within a three-year period. Given that he had a limited income, his prostitution habit alone was a severe strain on his family.

Beginning with Bill's treatment for his alcoholism, his wife and four children became involved in therapy. Bill began to get reacquainted with his children. His wife continued a cold and distant hostility. Very seldom would she comment or become involved. She saw it clearly as his problem and that "things would change if he did." It was not until Bill revealed that he was also a rapist that things changed in the family. The pain was so great for Ginger, his wife, that she too came into therapy.

For a month, it was doubtful if the family would stay together. With serious effort by all involved, their relationship improved. After seventeen months in the program, the marriage was rewarding for both; Bill was staying straight in all of his addictions and had recently been made a supervisor in his company. Keys to the recovery were honesty, recognition of all the levels of addiction, and total family involvement. As an indication of how key these elements are, the following is an edited excerpt from Bill's autobiography of what he had done:

I think of all the Saturday and Sunday mornings that I would sneak off, sometimes in the afternoon or evenings. But the sneakiest way was before anybody got up. That way I did not have to explain where I was going—only the lie as to where I had been when I got back home. "Where have you been all morning or all day?" Some of the lies were, "Oh, I was over to a friend's house," sometimes even making up a friend. Or the countless times that I had car trouble and how hard and long it was to fix. If asked about the friend, it was somebody from work: "You would not know him, anyway you never met him." (Example of mud slide after hard rain; helped an imaginary friend fix a wall that caved in.) Sometimes I got mad because she asked where I was. I said, "None of your business."

There was countless times where I came to work late, left early or did not show up at all. I told my boss I was sick or something happened at home. Spending endless hours driving around. I would leave the house on the spur of the moment with a lie to get in my car and go.

I could be driving down the steet with good intentions. Just a thought on the sight of a pretty girl would get me going. I would tell myself it is not going to happen, but did not have any control to stop it. Completely powerless, a feeling of being taken over by a strong emotionally uncontrollable power that I did not understand. Afterwards, I would feel so ashamed of what I had done and then starting right in over again, maybe even staying out all night or even looking for a prostitute.

Sometimes after the prostitute and driving home thinking about the prostitute, it would start in all over again; just the thought. I would get home and wonder why I had done it. Then not knowing where I was at, what I had been doing. Or being caught by someone I knew or somebody else knew, like the time my daughter's friend saw my picture at the police department. Plus, explaining where my money went when I had put it in the gas tank and all the nicks in the car.

I would sometimes wonder what the girl or woman thought or the remark they would make if they saw me, "Goddamn creep, queen, sex maniac, etc." You can well imagine how apart I was from my family because of the guilty feeling; shamefulness for time away from home; sad because of all of it. Angry at myself for not doing anything about it or being able to control it. Why am I this way, why me? How can a person live that way for ten to twelve years and face themself? Knowing what you are, the deep down truth crawling around in the back of your mind and the pit of your stomach. Everybody looks at you and you're not being able to look at them. Dear God help me.

To rape out of anger, passion, or lawlessness—as terrible as that is—does not constitute an addiction. There are some sexual addicts, however, for whom rape is part of a larger pattern. Once past our rage for what has been done, we can see rape as the most tragic extension of the addict's world.

Corollaries of the Levels of Addiction

The levels of addiction are arbitrary concepts. They serve, however, to show the wide range of behavior included in sexual addiction. While our discussion did not extend to every possible form of the addiction (e.g., bestiality, sadomasochism, and fetishism were omitted), the levels provide a basic strategy for understanding any sexually compulsive behavior. Most important, the levels make explicit the pattern created by the relationship between behaviors. See the chart, "Levels of Addiction," which follows on pages 54 and 55.

Many concepts are limited when applied to real life. The levels are no different. The incestuous father who combines bestiality with his dog with the sexual abuse of his daughters, the exhibitionist who spends time with his family in the nudist camp, the physician voyeur who does routine physicals as part of his practice—all are situations difficult to assess within the three levels. The value of the levels of addiction remains in their ability to underline the patterns of compulsive sexuality.

Just as the levels serve as a basic premise about the extent of addiction, there are five corollaries which follow that are critical to understanding the addiction. Each of the five must be recognized if the levels of addiction are to be useful tools in the assessment of any individual's addiction.

Corollary One: The sexual addiction of each level is painful.

The pain at each level is very real. The problem is that the public, addicts, and others dismiss the pain—but for different reasons at different levels. A macho society would perceive an unending string of lovers and prostitutes as simply having a good time. Level One behavior may even be envied or, at the minimum, regarded as normal but not as painful. Similarily, the nuisance offenders of Level Two are dismissed as pathetic and harmless or as the object of jokes (e.g., "flasher" jokes), but not as haunted, wounded, or broken people. Level Three behavior engenders such immediate rage that rapists, molesters, and incestuous fathers justifiably receive no quarter. There is much compassion for the victim, but no sense of the desperation of the addict.

Several years ago there was an episode of the TV show "Police Woman" which illustrated the stereotypic ways in which the pain of the addiction is dismissed. The plot of the story was about the chase and capture of two rapists. The rapists were brothers who were portrayed as cruel, vicious low-life types who by any viewer's standards would deserve the very worst.

In the midst of the chase, a sub-plot emerged designed for comic relief. Into the station walked a man who had been pinching women on elevators and could not stop. In desperation, he turned himself in. The contrast was intended to be comical. However, addicts who have thought of turning themselves in as a way out of their predicament had to find the episode disconcerting. Addicts can only guess at how they will be accepted by authorities.

Pathos, rage, and idealization of the male sexual role—all obscure the addict's pain. Without a sense of the loneliness, shame, and despair, none of the levels of sexual compulsiveness can be appreciated as an addiction.

Corollary Two: Deviant behavior does not necessarily indicate the presence of addiction.

Throughout this chapter, a constant theme has been that a pattern is necessary for addiction to exist. Rape and incest, for example, are tragic, but they are not necessarily the result of addiction. Deviancy, however, does involve risk. Risk does seem to be one of the prime ingredients to the mood-altering addictive process. To violate cultural and legal norms can enhance the sexual excitement. Risk, which is involved in the violation, is

LEVEL OF ADDICTION	BEHAVIOR	CULTURAL STANDARDS
Level One	Masturbation, heterosexual relationships, pornography, prostitution, and homosexuality	Depending on behavior, activities are seen as acceptable or tolerable. Some specific behaviors such as prostitution and homosexuality are sources of controversy.
Level Two	Exhibitionism, voyeurism, indecent phone calls, and indecent liberties.	None of these behaviors is acceptable.
Level Three	Child molestation, incest, and rape.	Each behavior represents a profound violation of cultural boundaries.

ADDICTION

LEGAL CONSEQUENCES/ RISKS	VICTIM	PUBLIC OPINION OF ADDICTION
Sanctions against those behaviors, when illegal, are ineffectively and randomly enforced. Low priority for enforcement officials generates minimal risk for addict.	These behaviors are perceived as victimless crimes. However, victimization and exploitation are often components.	Public attitudes are characterized by ambivalence or dislike. For some behaviors such as prostitution there is a competing negative hero image of glamorous decadence.
Behaviors are regarded as nuisance offenses. Risk is involved since offenders, when observed, are actively prosecuted.	There is always a victim.	Addict is perceived as pathetic and sick but harmless. Often these behaviors are the objects of jokes which dismiss the pain of the addict.
Extreme legal consequences create high-risk situations for the addict.	There is always a victim.	Public becomes outraged. Perpetrators are seen by many as sub-human and beyond help.

central to the escalation process so often described by addicts. Therefore, the presence of deviant behavior warrants exploring the possibility of sexual addiction.

Corollary Three: All three levels of addiction transcend personality, gender, and socio-economic status.

At this time, it is difficult to make descriptive statements about sexual addicts with empirical certainty. We do not know, for example, how many addicts there are in general, let alone how many addicts within specific levels. There is no survey technique which can guarantee total candor about sexual behavior across the levels. Nor has there been, heretofore, an integrating concept—such as addiction—which makes connections within patterns of behavior for reseachers to use. Finally, studies of sexual compulsiveness most often are done within the criminal justice system. Obviously, total honesty brings risk in that situation. The stories of members of Twelve Step groups and the case histories of those who have been forced into treatment or who have sought help voluntarily are our best sources to date. Their experiences suggest that the addiction has few limits, transcending personality, gender and socio-economic status.

Personality studies of people with sexually compulsive behavior have had only limited success in specifying personality characteristics.[6] Psychological test data, clinical observation, and case studies usually indicate there is no outstanding similarity in personality factors. Convincing arguments are difficult to find for any kind of general personality type even within a specific category of compulsivity. In addition, researchers often have only small groups to study, do not look at overall sexual patterns, and ignore the presence of multiple addictions. Research is further complicated by the delusional thought processes of addicts who, in fact, are not aware of the extent of their problems. A long time elapses before recovering addicts have clarity, let alone before they are able and willing to describe their past situations to others.

Like alcoholism, the sexual addiction may include many variations of personality and even personality disorders. As suggested in chapter one, concurrent emotional illness is often part of the addict's world. The levels of addiction highlight the fact that no longer can we generalize about the shy flasher, the hard-core rapist, the sex-starved john, or the socially inept incestuous parent. Sexual addiction can flourish in the most competent, attractive, and charming people as well as in the most retiring, repulsive, and ill.

Nor can we assume that sexual addiction is a lower class phenomenon. The case examples used in the writing of this book represent a broad spectrum of class, profession, and educational experience. Within the public media, there is a constant parade of key public figures who have been exposed for their sexual compulsiveness. Within a few months of this writing,

—a high-ranking federal official was arrested for sexual activities in a Washington, D.C., bookstore.

—a state supreme court judge, nationally recognized for his legal scholarship, was exposed by a television news team for his activities with teenage homosexual prostitutes.

—one of the aerospace engineers who helped design the space shuttle was cited for incest with his children.

—the president and chief executive officer of one of the largest family-owned manufacturing companies was exposed as the central figure in a large child pornography network.

—a minister and high-ranking official of a large Protestant denomination was arrested for exhibitionism.

The sensationalism which surrounds these cases obscures the fact that the consequences of sexual addiction may fall harder on addicts with less money and access to legal assistance. Contrast the sexual activities of J.R. Ewing of the television series "Dallas" with a working man who has only enough money to pick up street "hookers." The latter is clearly less protected. Professionals are beginning to wonder if the extent of sexual compulsiveness among those with more resources has been underestimated. For example, professionals are now reporting to the National Center on Child Abuse and Neglect (NCCAN) an increasing number of cases of sexual abuse among middle and upper income families.

The levels of addiction also provide a more complete perspective of the sexual addiction for women. Men are clearly perceived as capable of being obsessive about sex. Because of the sexual exploitation of women, the image of women alleviating their pain through sexual obsession is more rare. Yet, our media is filled with examples like Mrs. Robinson in *The Graduate*, Theresa in *Looking for Mr. Goodbar*, or the desperate women in *American Gigolo*. Sexual compulsiveness exists for women on each level of the addiction. The woman who repeatedly uses objects to masturbate to the point of injury, the woman "flasher" who hikes her dress and opens the car door to expose herself to passing men, and the woman who has been sexual with four out of her six children—all can share a common addictive process.

There are special problems for women addicts. There are the risks of violence and pregnancy. There is the double standard for the sexual behavior of women. There are the conflicting messages of cultural norms. A woman in a bikini or a low-cut gown is idolized and a stripper is degraded. Men addicts ask, "Why, when a man looks at a woman in a window, he is a voyeur, and when a woman looks at a man in a window, he is an exhibitionist?" Setting aside the rage for women implicit in the question, it does raise the problem of public attitudes towards women.

Consider the woman who exposes herself in public. The reactions will probably be less punitive than for a man. Yet, given the cultural role of women as guardians of sexual morality, the shame is greater. Similar dynamics exist for women who have multiple affairs or are sexual with children. Their recovery is made harder because of the messages incorporated in their belief systems about how a woman "should" be. Even to admit there is a sexual problem is more difficult. To reject the reality of sexual addiction for women is to perpetuate the sexism which has prevented women with other addictions from receiving help in the past.

Corollary Four: Sexual behaviors within and between levels reinforce one another.

Within the levels of behaviors, the addict will shift from one behavior to another depending on availability, risk, and situation. The salesman feels safer entering a massage parlor or bookstore on the road than at home. Masturbating while looking at pornography can suffice when the addict has failed to make the evening pick-up at the local bars. The addict who makes indecent phone calls and is worried about arrest can now call a phone service. One-half hour of explicit sexual conversation with a young woman while masturbating can be charged to his credit card.

An example of how behavior can shift within the addictive cycle was shared by a woman who worked in a massage parlor. She reported that recently there had been a rape of one of the masseuses in the place she worked. When she went to the police station to examine mugshots of sex offenders, she was stunned to discover that she was able to recognize a large number of the pictures—they were her clients. It was shortly after that she entered therapy.

Corollary Five: Sexual behavior in each level is connected with behaviors due to other kinds of addiction.

The pattern of sexual behavior is not complete unless the reinforcement of other compulsive behaviors is counted. Overeating, working, and drinking or abusing drugs are integral to the addict's pattern. This is true, for example, when:

—working until exhausted justifies sexual compulsiveness as "deserved."

—drinking and cruising are mutually intoxicating.

—binge eating routinely follows a visit to a porno shop.

—gambling and prostitution are an irresistible combination.

Just as the sexual behaviors on each level reinforce each other, other addictions play an important role in conjunction with each other. The interaction between addictions may be at just one level. Consider the incestuous father who is also an alcoholic. His compulsive masturbation, use of pornography, or prostitutes did not necessarily have to involve drinking. Yet, every time he was sexual with his daughter he was also drunk. The two addictions come together at Level Three, but not Level One. Addicts must discern the total pattern in order to understand their powerlessness and unmanageability.

Addiction As a System

Traditionally, sexual compulsiveness has been described in a very linear fashion. Behavior was divided into types and categories with each having its own origin. Exhibitionists were one way, incestuous fathers were another, and the unfaithful spouse yet another. Undoubtedly each behavior has unique characteristics. The difficulty in gathering data plus the shame and denial system of the addict perpetuate the idea that each individual category is unique. However, for true addicts there is a common link in sexual obsession.

The addiction is truly a system where behavior is interdependent. There are constantly shifting patterns which weave together the various levels of sexually compulsive behavior and which may include other addictions and emotional disorders. The system operates on a repetitive rhythm. The driving force for each cycle comes from a faulty belief system translated through delusional thought patterns. In general, systems are self-perpetuating and the sexual addiction as a system does just that. The completion of each cycle confirms that belief system and the impaired thinking. Out of the validation of the beliefs a new and stronger cycle is born. The behavior, then, becomes intensified within Level One, and sometimes extended to Levels Two and Three.

A key component of the addict's system is the larger network of family and loved ones who are part of the addictive cycle. Their behavior too emerges in patterns which interact and cycle. The family's participation in the addict's world is the focus of the next chapter.

3

The Family and the Addict's World

James Cermak's attorney, Fred Bruno, argued that sentencing Cermak for each sex offense would be like sentencing an alcoholic for each drink he takes.

Minneapolis Tribune
January 20, 1982

News of the Cermak brothers grabbed the public's attention for almost a year. Few tales were as grim as the unfolding story of their sexual abuse of a large number of children from their rural Minnesota town. The children included all of their own children plus others from the community. Most were elementary or junior high age youngsters, the youngest being the three-year-old son of James Cermak. Both brothers, James and John, were sentenced to forty years in prison, neither being eligible for parole for at least twenty-six years.

Central to the Cermaks' activities was playing something they called "the game." Done in their homes or hotel rooms, "the game" started with the children sitting on a bed in a circle with no clothes on. They were then asked to perform sexual acts with one another. The game concluded with the Cermaks being sexual with the children including oral intercourse. Children were told they were "naughty" if they did not play and were threatened with physical violence if they resisted.

The number of children involved, the sexual violation and the emotional vulnerability of the children, and the cruelty of the Cermak brothers generated public outrage. The brothers' parents, Stanley and Alice, protested that the children had been "programmed" by the prosecuting attorney and denied the allegations. Yet, over 130 pieces of evidence were introduced including about seventy instant photographs of the children in obscene poses or performing sexual acts. Even the Cermak brothers acknowledged the depth of the tragedy. John Cermak was so remorseful that suicidal feelings were a problem. James Cermak told the judge, "I'm sorry for the things I have done and I'm only twenty-six years old and I definitely need help."[1]

Hardly had public outrage started to subside when shocking new revelations appeared in the media. Beverly and Jillayne Cermak, the wives of James and John, were also being charged with child rape. They had both played "the game." Beverly was accused of having sex with seven children and forcing them to perform sex acts with other children over a two-and-a-half-year period. Jillayne was charged with eighteen counts of sexual abuse of children, nine of which were counts of first degree criminal sexual conduct. Both Jillayne and Beverly were accused of aiding and abetting their husbands.

The Cermak story is classic if extreme: the denial of the grandparents in their efforts to protect the family secrets, the seemingly unending series of disclosures which gave testimony as to how sexual obsession prevailed in the life style of the family, the profound feelings of remorse, regret, and helplessness of the offenders, the loyalty of children who did not wish to testify against their parents, spouses who collaborated, and a public who chose to see the tragic series of events as isolated, bizarre, and unique.

Sexual compulsiveness, like all addictions, rests in a complex web of family relationships. The Cermaks are unique only in the degree to which their addiction escalated and the amount of publicity they got. Among the Cermak tragedies is the fact that each of the children involved has a high potential for participating in an addictive relationship as an adult. This chapter and the following are designed to show how the sexual addiction is a family illness and to trace how the abuse of children makes them vulnerable to addictive relationships. Most important will

be to show the relationship of the family to the world of the
addict described in chapters one and two.

The Role of the Family

Sexual addiction, as a family illness, parallels almost every
other emotional and addictive disorder. For the past twenty
years professionals in many disciplines have been documenting
the family as a "system"—regulated by rules and roles, understanding and misunderstanding. The family system has the capacity to sustain unity, establish the distance between family
members, allow individual uniqueness, and produce organized
effort. The family, above all, has a range of options available
to maintain balance. Being balanced for family members makes
them feel normal. Not always, but sometimes, this means keeping things the same even if they are painful.

Suicide, schizophrenia, alcoholism, runaways—all are part
of the family epic. For example, in alcoholism, treatment of
the spouse alone has been shown to promote recovery in the
alcoholic. Now, throughout the ranks of specialists in addiction,
treating the entire family is regarded as critical. It is recognized
that the more members involved, the higher the recovery rate.
Moreover, spouses, parents, and children, by virtue of their
participation in the family insanity, have a right to recovery
for themselves.

Whatever the disorder, family members are often unaware
of their own pain. They very clearly do not understand their
contribution to the family drama. A sign of the family members'
delusion is their deep-seated conviction that they had little to
do with it. If only that other person:

— would stop drinking
— could control eating

— could keep his or her feet on the ground
— had not run away
— were not always depressed
— were not so obsessed with sex
— could manage life better
— were more responsible
— could keep a job
— would grow up and stop acting like a child.

A more severe delusion is when the family does not even acknowledge there is a problem. Therein may be the ultimate tragedy of the Cermak grandparents who protested that the children were programmed by the prosecuting attorney. By maintaining the public image of the family, the family member can hold the pain at bay until the consequences come crashing in. The ultimate revelation in the Cermak case came when the public learned that James and John Cermak, the accused, had been victimized by their father. Both grandparents were also accused of being sexual with their grandchildren. Family denial appears to be accelerated in the sexual addiction because of the shame and moral connotations of sexual behavior. In that sense, sexual addiction as a family dysfunction is different from other family illnesses. Yet, the task remains for each member of the family to search out his or her individual part in the family predicament. All first efforts in understanding one's part in the family begin with the family in which one was raised. Part of acknowledging true powerlessness for both the addict and the concerned persons starts with the recognition that the roots of the addiction may, in fact, span generations.

Many of the stories throughout this book indicate the transmission of sexual addiction from one generation to the next. The question to answer now is how this transfer occurs.

There are four factors in a child's development which ultimately become part of the sexual addiction. They are:

Self-image	— how children perceive themse.
Relationships	— how children perceive their relationships with others.
Needs	— how children perceive their own needs.
Sexuality	— how children perceive their own sexual feelings and needs.

These perceptions ultimately become "core beliefs" central to the addictive system. They are conclusions which can govern the choices and behaviors during the child's adult life. In this chapter, we will focus on how the process of developing core beliefs unfolds for the addict. In the next chapter, the evolving core beliefs of other family members will be examined.

Self-image and Relationships

Morris was an exhibitionist. He had initially started to expose himself as a teenager, but exposure remained only as an off-and-on problem until his early forties. Until then, he was involved in nudist clubs, a few affairs, and with numerous prostitutes. The crisis for the family occurred when Morris started to expose himself to a neighbor woman next door. Then he started to expose to passersby. The experience was extremely horrifying for the family who had to suffer neighborhood outrage, police harassment, and the sale, at a loss, of their home of ten years. The more his wife Linda would try to control his behavior, the worse it became. With both involved in therapy and a Twelve Step group for sexual compulsiveness, and with the move providing a fresh start, Morris was able to redirect his life.

As a child, Morris was raised by his alcoholic father. His mother left him at the age of six. While his father traveled, Morris was left at a boarding house run by two spinster sisters. He was the only child in the house, the rest of the residents being older men. The two sisters found numerous occasions to punish him with severe brutality. Punishment meant taking his clothes off and being beaten, especially around the genital area. After these session the old men would comfort the boy by masturbating him to sleep.

The two sisters set up traps for Morris to guarantee "punishment" sessions. For example, knowing that the Saturday matinee ended at three, they would tell the boy to return no later than 2:30 p.m. Obviously Morris would not be able to pass up the end of his movie and would arrive a half hour late. The punishment was, therefore, rationalized. The father would not believe the boy's stories and so Morris lived under these conditions from the age of six until he was ten and his father remarried. A significant part of Morris's therapy was to return to the small Illinois town in which these events took place and grieve over a lost childhood.

The story of Morris illustrates common antecedents to addiction. First, there is alcoholism in the family. Second, physical and emotional abuse accompany sexual abuse. Third, sexual experience is both humiliating and comforting. And fourth, the reality of the child is denied when the child's accounts of abuse are not taken seriously. All of these are potent contributors to the addiction as we shall see.

By far the most important factor, however, is a sense of having been abandoned. From a child's point of view, "you can abuse me, humiliate me, exploit me, and even not believe me, but by far the worst is if you don't even want me." Fear of abandonment is a constant theme in all addictions including alcoholism. Within the sexual addiction, it is especially powerful.

Abandonment has a thousand forms. Some forms are explicit such as Morris's mother leaving him at age six and his dad traveling. In some cases certain events are interpreted as abandonment. Corky, for example, was a twenty-year-old exhibitionist who was also chemically dependent. His mother died when Corky was thirteen. He started exposing himself almost immediately, the first arrest happening only a few months after her death. An important part of his therapy came when he was able to connect his exhibitionism to how alone he felt when his mother died.

Even the threat of abandonment can be potent. Reseachers Eist and Mandel describe how, within families where incest has occurred, "tremendous parental threats of abandonment were a most frequent technique employed by the parents to control or immobilize their children."[2] In writing about sexual compulsiveness, Julie Sherman has termed this phenomenon the "Coatlicue Complex" after the Aztec mother of the gods who symbolized "the power of life and death that each mother holds over her infant."[3] The sexual addiction receives its power from a fundamental concern for survival.

The first core belief of the addict is *I am basically a bad, unworthy person.* Abandonment means being unwanted. The child can only conclude that unwanted means unworthy and bad.

A good example was Art, a twenty-seven-year-old chemically dependent man whose sexual addiction included multiple relationships, exhibitionism, voyeurism, obscene calls, and eventually rape. When he was four years old, his mother left and his alcoholic father remarried. His father was a sexual addict and so were several uncles. Art writes in his autobiography about his life with his stepmother:

> My brother and I were pretty regular brats and we took a lot of sadistic and humiliating treatment from our mother. One of her favorite punishments was tying us to chairs. Sometimes she'd make us wear diapers. We were old enough to be extremely mortified by it. She made my brother play outside like that once.
>
> Another fun thing my mother did to me was to dress me up like a girl. She put make-up on me and curlers in my

69

hair and thought what a cute girl I would have made.

Obviously, with three boys she must have wanted a girl, but what a crummy thing to do, I went along with it but I felt really embarrassed.

I have a lot of hatred for women and a lot of it is from my mother. A lot of resentment came out—just that she wasn't my real mother. I guess I have some anger at my real mother for abandoning me even though I understand she tried to get custody.

After she ran out of ways to punish us we had to sit and think of our own punishments. I spent a lot of time thinking of different ways to be punished. This is where I got a lot of my guilt and shame and when I learned to be self-punishing.

Note again the themes of abuse, punishment, and humiliation, as well as abandonment. The more prevalent these elements are, the more compelling the addiction.

A second core belief comes from the first core belief about the child being a bad person. Because of personal unworthiness, the child believes: *No one would love me as I am.* Relationships with others become more tenuous the deeper this belief is. Children grow up believing that no one will accept them unconditionally. People will not be there; they cannot be trusted or depended on. If they do want a relationship, it is because they want something—not because they care. There will always be a price to pay. Minimally, there will be something that must be overlooked, ignored, or denied. To be close will mean to lose reality or integrity somehow. So intimacy is avoided. As the child grows up, a personal front or public image designed to look good shields the emerging adult from the searching gaze of others which will lead to rejection.

Needs and Sexuality

Addicts report that as children they felt desperately lonely, lost, and unprotected. Not only was there a lack of nurturing, but there was no one to show them how to take care of themselves or keep from harm. Not being able to count on—depend upon—the adults in one's life to meet needs is a key element in addiction. As the child matures, there begins a search for that which is dependable—something that you can trust to make you feel better. Trust and dependency are the issues which determine personal strength and confidence or vulnerability to enslaving addiction. For in the lonely search for something or someone to depend on—which has already excluded parents—a child can start to find those things which always comfort, which always feel good, which always are there, and which always do what they promise. For some, alcohol and drugs are the answer. For others it is food. And there is always sex—which usually costs nothing and nobody else can regulate.

This choice stems from the addict's third core belief which is about needs: *My needs are never going to be met if I have to depend upon others.* In healthy families, children have a deep sense that their parents care for them as opposed to abandoning them.

Healthy parenting includes touching, loving, affirming and guiding. The child feels cared for even when struggling with rules and limits. Trust in one's self, as well as trust of others, emerges in that relationship.

When a child's exploration of sexuality goes beyond discovery to routine self-comforting because of the lack of human care, there is potential for addiction. Sex becomes confused with comforting and nurturing. Moreover, the assumption is made that everyone else feels and acts the same. Therefore, to feel secure means to be sexual.

Consequently, the child's relationships with people have the potential of being replaced with an addictive relationship with sexuality. Addiction is a relationship—a pathological relationship in which sexual obsession replaces people. And it can start very early. The final core belief of the addict emerges clearly: *Sex is my most important need.*

The kinds of childhood situations described here are further complicated when the children are surrounded by negative rules, messages, and judgments about sex. When addicts and their spouses study their families of origin, they are flooded with memories of events where they were told that being sexual was bad, or worse, that they were bad for being sexual.

When children's primary source of comfort is sex, and yet they are told by those whose judgments count the most that to be sexual is perverse, the conclusions they make about themselves are clear. They are unlikeable. They need to hide that central part of themselves which others will despise. Rather than repressing the sexual behaviors, they hide them or keep them secret. Needing to keep that central part of themselves secret adds to the pain and loneliness—which, in turn, creates a need for comfort, making the sexual fix that much more necessary.

The fusion between sex and nurturing is cemented if the children are victims of sexual abuse. Level Two and Level Three addicts are almost always sexually abused as children. Parents, clergy, older siblings, relatives, physicians, friends, teachers, babysitters—a wide range of people have the potential of exploiting a child. Children learn from the important adults in their lives how to have a significant human relationship. Once a person has learned how to have a relationship with other people, then the sexual component can be added as a special expression of a special relationship. If the parents or significant adults are sexual with the child, the young person will always have difficulty sorting out sexuality and relationship.

"The Abuse Checklist," following on pages 74 and 75, is intended as a guide to help addicts identify sexual, physical, and emotional abuse which occurred in their childhoods.

A sexual addict exploring his early years can pick out the most blatant examples of victimization. There are, however, a number of factors which can obscure the victimization. For example, professionals such as clergy, physicians, teachers, and therapists who are sexual within the context of their profession are hard to detect if their intentions are not explicit. Thus, a child who feels "funny" about the physical exam he or she received decides that it was imagination. The feeling or intuition, however, may have been very accurate.

Sexual compulsivity also obscures victimization. Addicts consider any sexual contact as a victory. Addicts commonly discover, as they share their sexual history with other addicts, that many of their early sexual experiences were exploitive. They learn, for example, that for a fourteen-year-old boy to be sexual with a woman in her thirties is for him to be abused. Yet the boy doesn't identify this as abuse. When it feels good, it is hard to notice. From the addict's point of view as an adolescent, it was a "score."

One of the hardest barriers to overcome for addicts in understanding their own victimization is family loyalty. Children are incredibly loyal—even under the worst conditions. Not only parents, uncles, cousins, but even stepparents and family friends are not to be betrayed. These family bonds are reinforced by a rule which says the "family takes care of its own problems." Like all victims, addicts have difficulty in breaking the family "secret" to others.

For those addicts who have experienced family sexual abuse, breaking the secret is the most explicit way to trace the transmission of the sexual addiction from one generation to the next.

One addict who, in addition to compulsive use of prostitutes and extra-marital affairs, had been incestuous with two of his three sons, made a major breakthrough in recalling his own childhood. His father told him when he was a child that the doctor had asked that he manipulate his son's foreskin in order to

THE ABUSE

The following checklist and worksheet will help you assess the extent to which you were abused in your own childhood experience. Read over each of the three categories of abuse (sexual, physical, emotional). Fill in the information in spaces next to the items which apply to you.

FORM OF ABUSE	AGE
A. Sexual Abuse	
Suggestive flirtatiousness	_____
Propositioning	_____
Inappropriate holding, kissing	_____
Fondling of sexual parts	_____
Masturbation	_____
Oral sex	_____
Forceful sexual activity	_____
Other	_____
B. Physical Abuse	
Shoving	_____
Slapping, hitting	_____
Scratches, bruises	_____
Burns	_____
Cuts, wounds	_____
Broken bones, fractures	_____
Damage to organs	_____
Permanent injury	_____
Other	_____
C. Emotional Abuse	
Neglect	_____
Harassment, malicious tricks	_____
Blackmail	_____
Unfair punishments	_____
Cruel or degrading tasks	_____
Cruel confinement	_____
Abandonment	_____
Other	_____

CHECKLIST

For each type of abuse, record the information to the best of your memory:

Age: How old were you when it started?

Abusing Persons: Who abused you? Father, stepfather, mother, stepmother, adult relative, adult friend, adult neighbor, professional person, brother or sister, or stranger?

Frequency: How often did it happen? Daily, two to three times a week, weekly, monthly, or occasionally?

ABUSING PERSON   **FREQUENCY**

insure its flexibility when he became an adult. This manipulation led to frequent sexual contact between father and son. When the father's father (grandfather of the sons) was brought into therapy, he admitted that in fact he had not talked to the doctor, but had learned it from *his* father. How did the great-grandfather know? From his father. The special irony in all of this was that the addict had been circumcised.

Children do not have to be victimized in order to be affected by the victimization. A son who lives in the house in which his sisters are victimized is clearly at risk. Similarly, being in the presence of sexual compulsivity of any form has its impact and creates vulnerability to addiction. Addicts frequently discover that their behavior parallels that of their parents or relatives. The addict—as well as his spouse—absolutely needs to know that there were affairs or prostitutes or compulsive acting out in the preceding generations.

Sexual compulsivity in previous generations is usually a well-guarded secret. The addicts believe they are the only ones who are sexually compulsive which increases their shame. What they do not know is that the judgment and negative rules around sex originate in the obsession of the parent who fears that the compulsivity he or she has experienced might happen to the child. Unwittingly, the parents' efforts to contain sexual activity add a key negative catalyst to the addiction, as the previous generation did.

The cosmic observer would have an epic spectacle of generations of sexual addicts all lost in their own loneliness and compulsivity. Lonely as children, they are lonely as parents. Unable to admit they need help to make things different, they create the very same empty environment for their own children.

The Core Beliefs and the Addict's World

All addicts can find elements of their sexual compulsiveness in their early years. Even if no overt experiences of abuse exist, the fundamental self-doubt and distrust of others lay waiting as potential factors in addiction. Examples of all four core beliefs can be identified in the addict's childhood. However, when the addiction takes over, an addict's life varies according to individual life experience. For some, the compulsiveness starts early such as in the case of the young exhibitionist who started exposing himself right after his mother's death. For others, compulsiveness emerges full force in adult years usually in response to stress and anxiety. For every addict the common denominator is the addictive system described in chapter one. The addict's belief system lays the foundation for impaired thinking which supports the addictive cycle (preoccupation, ritualization, pattern of sex and behavior, depression). The resulting unmanageability and powerlessness confirm and deepen the core beliefs. At that point, when the belief system, including the core beliefs, is intensified, the addictive system becomes fully engaged.

The core beliefs which were part and parcel of the addict's growing up become central to the addict's world as an adult. Each core belief contributes to the disconnection between the interior world the addict experiences with its pain and shame, and the exterior image the addict projects to keep the secret world safe. The addict lives in constant personal "jeopardy" dreading the moment when the secret world will be unmasked. The addict becomes more isolated as the secret life grows. Family and friends become more peripheral. Loved ones struggle with the increasing alienation, as well as a mounting number of discrepancies between what the addict says and does. They cannot penetrate into the addict's secret world. Each core belief adds to the barriers protecting the internal world.

The belief *I am basically a bad, unworthy person* structures the emotional foundations of the addict's world. Addicts conclude from their family experiences that they are not worthwhile persons. Feelings of inadequacy and failure predominate. Addicts even see humiliation and degradation as justified or deserved. The desperate struggle around sexual compulsivity absolutely confirms this belief and enhances feelings of low self-worth. Addicts are committed to hiding the secret reality of their addiction at all costs because of their unworthiness. Yet, it guides almost all behavior and decisions.

Addicts create a front of "normalcy" to hide their sense of inadequacy. They may even appear grandiose and full of exaggerated self-importance. The front contrasts with actions which appear degrading or self-defeating or both. Others see decisions or behaviors as irrational, unfathomable, or even self-destructive, but not "normal."

Close friends and family members become angry and frustrated with the addict's egocentric quality especially when there is insensitivity to others. They are troubled at what looks like destructive or curious behavior which does not fit the image the addict projects.

The belief *No one would love me as I am* also sustains the secret world. Addicts continue to believe that everyone would abandon them if the truth were known. Consequently, they have a constant fear of being vulnerable or dependent on others. Addicts perceive their behavior as so bad that everything that goes wrong becomes their fault. Addicts assume responsibility for all the pain in loved ones. Honest guilt and remorse cannot be expressed because they would require honesty about behavior. Addicts progressively become more isolated from normal contact with family and friends.

Yet, addicts create the image of being in charge of life and in no need of help. They appear unaffected by any problems, but will often do extreme or indulgent things as if making up for something. No explanation is offered, however. Some addicts may continue to be charming and sociable, but all addicts become "unreachable" personally as they close off all avenues of vulnerability.

Significant persons in the addict's life start to feel cut out, pushed away, useless, neglected, and unnecessary. They become confused: the addict makes seemingly generous gestures, but lacks any personal warmth or presence. The family and friends feel angry, hurt, and rejected in response to the addict's contradictory behavior.

My needs are never going to be met if I have to depend upon others is the belief which provides the addiction with its driving power. The survival needs of the child are transformed into the desperation of the addict's interior world. Basically, addicts feel unloved and unlovable which means their needs will be unmet. The resulting rage becomes internalized as depression, resentment, self-pity, and even suicidal feelings. Because they have no confidence others will love them, addicts become calculating, strategizing, manipulative, and ruthless. Rules and laws are designed for people who are lovable. Those who are unlovable have to survive in other ways.

The addict's rage about unmet needs in the past prevents the possibility of expressing needs now, because addicts anticipate they will be rejected. Consequently, addicts appear not to want or need anything at a human level. They are purposely unclear about their intentions in relationships which makes for a kind of seductive behavior, i.e., they try to be affirmed or cared for without expressing that they need it so they will not be rejected. Addicts make extensive efforts to show how respectable and law-abiding they are.

As consequences to the addiction begin to emerge, those who are close start to see the double life, the Jekyll and Hyde, in the addict's world. The addict's ups and downs remain difficult to understand. Worse, family and friends begin to distrust and disbelieve the addict. Things appear to be so smooth yet the intuition is they are not. Inconsistencies between the addict's public and private lives confirm these intuitions.

The belief which makes sexual obsession the focus of the addiction is *Sex is my most important need.* The addict continues to confuse nurturing and sex. Support, care, affirmation, and love are all sexualized. Absolute terror of life without sex combines with feelings of unworthiness for having such intense sexual desires. Sexual activity never meets the need for love and care, but it continues to be seen as the only avenue. The addict has a high need to control all situations in an effort to guarantee sex. Yet there is a secret fear of being sexually out of control. Addicts promise themselves to stop or limit sexual behavior because of this fear.

Sexual obsession pervades the addict's life style and behavior. They make the maximum effort to insure all possible sexual oppportunities. All levels of addictive behavior directly reflect the need to control sexual access. In other words, multiple affairs, prostitution, exhibitionism, voyeurism, incest, rape, etc., have in common the goal of protecting "the source of supply." Seeking degrading or humiliating sexual experiences simply extends internal feelings of unworthiness. However, addicts profess extreme sexual propriety even to the extent of moral self-righteousness about sexual matters. Cover-ups, lies, and deceptions are made to conceal personal sexual behavior.

The addict's protestations of high sexual morality are like a smoke screen, obscuring the impact of sexual obsession. Friends and family tend to reject suspicions of sexual compulsivity because of the addict's "values." However, as evidence of powerless behavior and unmanageability mount, these persons are confused because they do not know what to believe. In addition, they do not wish to intervene in something so personal. Finally, the distance and lack of personal connection take their toll. Since few feel close enough to say anything, they choose the other option which is to withdraw.

The following chart, "The World of the Sexual Addict," summarizes how the core beliefs learned in childhood continue to influence the interior and exterior portions of the addict's world as well as the family members and friends of the addict.

The sexual addiction clearly has its roots in the family life of the addict. The role of the family does not end there, however. The family continues to play an integral part in the addictive system. This part is called co-addiction. When family members become so involved in one addiction they participate in the illness, they are called co-addicts. They are the focus of the next chapter.

CORE BELIEF 1
SELF-IMAGE: I am basically a bad,
unworthy person.

Interior World

Addicts conclude from their family experiences that they are not worthwhile persons. Feelings of inadequacy and failure predominate. Addicts often see humiliation and degradation as justified or deserved. The desperate struggle around sexual compulsivity absolutely confirms this belief and enhances feelings of low self-worth. Addicts are committed to hiding the secret reality of their addiction at all costs because of their unworthiness. Yet, the addiction guides almost all behavior and decisions.

Exterior World

Addicts create a front of "normalcy" to hide their sense of inadequacy. They may even appear grandiose and full of exaggerated self-importance. As consequences to behaviors emerge, the front contrasts with actions which seem to be degrading and self-defeating or both. Others see decisions or behaviors as irrational, incomprehensible, or even self-destructive, but not "normal."

Family and Friends

Close friends and family members become angry and frustrated with addicts' egocentricity, especially when there is insensitivity to others. Not knowing the interior world of an addict, they are troubled by what looks like destructive or curious behavior which does not fit the image the addicts project.

SEXUAL ADDICT

CORE BELIEF 2
RELATIONSHIPS: No one would love me
as I am.

Interior World

Addicts believe that everyone would abandon them if the truth were known. They have a constant fear of being dependent on others. Addicts perceive their sexual behavior as so bad that everything becomes their "fault." Addicts assume responsibility for all the pain in loved ones. Honest guilt and remorse cannot be expressed because that would require honesty about behavior. Addicts become progressively more isolated.

Exterior World

Addicts create image of being in charge of life and in no need of help. They appear unaffected by any problem, but will often do extreme or indulgent things as if making up for something. No explanation is offered, however. Some addicts may continue to be charming and sociable, but all addicts become "unreachable" personally as they close off all avenues of vulnerability.

Family and Friends

Significant persons in the addicts' lives start to feel pushed away, useless, neglected, and unnecessary. They become confused at seemingly generous gestures, but the absence of any personal warmth or presence. Anger and hurt accumulate with a sense of abandonment in reaction to addicts' irresponsible behavior.

THE WORLD OF THE

CORE BELIEF 3
NEEDS: My needs are never going to be met
if I have to depend on others.

Interior World

Addicts feel unloved and unlovable which means other people cannot be depended on to love them, so their needs will not be met. The resulting rage becomes internalized as depression, resentment, self-pity, and even suicidal feelings. Because they have no confidence in others' love, addicts become calculating, strategizing, manipulative, and ruthless. Rules and laws are made for people who are lovable. Those who are unlovable survive in other ways.

Exterior World

Addicts' rage about unmet needs in the past prevents the possibility of expressing needs now because they anticipate being rejected. Addicts appear not to want or need anything. They are purposely unclear about their intentions in relationships and are thus seductive in behavior, i.e., they try to be affirmed or cared for without expressing that they need it so they will not risk rejection. Addicts make extensive efforts to show how respectable and law-abiding they are.

Family and Friends

Those who are close start to see the double life, the Jekyll and Hyde, in the addicts' world. The addicts' ups and downs remain difficult to understand. Worse, distrust and disbelief in the addicts begin. Things appear to be so smooth, yet the intuition is they are not. Inconsistencies between the addicts' public and private lives confirm these intuitions.

84

CORE BELIEF 4
SEXUALITY: Sex is my most important need.

Interior World

Addicts confuse nurturing and sex. Support, care, affirmation, and love are all sexualized. Absolute terror of life without sex combines with feelings of unworthiness for such intense sexual desires. Sexual activity never meets the need for love and care, but continues to be seen as the only avenue to do so. Addicts have a high need to control all situations in an effort to guarantee sex. Yet, there is a secret fear of being sexually out of control. Addicts promise themselves to stop or limit sexual behavior because of this fear.

Exterior World

Sexual obsession pervades life style and behavior. Addicts make maximum effort to insure all possible sexual opportunities. Addicts at all levels of addictive behavior feel the need to control sexual access; that is, addicts involved in prostitution, exhibitionism, voyeurism, incest, etc., have in common the goal of protecting the "source of supply." Seeking degrading or humiliating sexual experiences simply extends internal feelings of unworthiness. Addicts publicly profess extreme sexual propriety, however, even to the extent of moral self-righteousness about sexual matters. Cover-ups, lies, and deceptions are made to conceal personal sexual behavior.

Family and Friends

The addicts' protestations of high sexual morality obscure the impact of sexual obsession on friends and families. Close family and friends tend to reject suspicions of sexual compulsivity because of addicts' "values." As evidence of powerlessness over behavior and unmanageability mount, these persons become confused, not knowing what to believe. In addition, they do not wish to intervene in something so personal. Since they don't feel close enough to become involved, they choose the other option which is to withdraw.

4

Co-addiction

Ruth Coe, the mother of convicted rapist, Frederick Coe, was charged Friday with hiring a man she did not know was an undercover police officer to kill the prosecutor who tried her son and the judge who sentenced him to life in prison.

Spokane Review
November 21, 1981

The plight of Ruth Coe is a tragic example of the family illness which affects those who care for the sexually compulsive. Her son, Frederick Coe, was accused of being the "South Hill Rapist." Thirty-seven rapes were attributed to this rapist who employed a highly ritualized strategy of following women as they left busses to walk to their homes. Coe was given life plus seventy-five years on conviction for four of the rapes. During the trial, Ruth Coe gained a certain notoriety for her testimony. She had elaborate alibis for her son including a description of how she and her son had searched "together" for the real South Hill rapist by following busses. The testimony plus her attempt at violent revenge creates a profile of a woman in profound pain about her son.

The tragedy of the Coe family was intensified by the fact that Gordon Coe, the father, was the highly respected managing editor for the *Spokane Daily Chronicle,* one of the two metropolitan papers. Among the issues that emerged was whether the press, particularly the rival *Spokane Review,* handled the case so sensationally that it prejudiced the trial of Fred Coe. Closely related was the issue of whether Ruth Coe was a victim of police entrapment. The heightened publicity obscured the very real pain and powerlessness of the Coe family.

Ruth Coe at the age of sixty-one was still active, aggressive, and attractive. She had distinguished herself in her college teaching as well as community activities. She clearly had violated her own value system in her offering the undercover agent money. The psychologist who examined her reported her to be a woman in "deep grief." While Ruth Coe may or may not be a co-addict, grief and addiction have something in common: denial. One of the first reactions of a grieving person is the denial of the loss of the loved one. The loss of relationship because of addictive involvement generates all those basic human processes involved at separation: hope, denial, anger, despair, and loneliness. A grieving person resolves pain by acknowledging the loss and reconnecting with others. Losing a loved one to addiction, however, has the potential of keeping one stuck in the early stages of grief never coming to resolution. The addict is still present in one's life even though the loss of the relationship is real.

Therein is the bind of the "co-addict," or the loved one or friend who becomes so involved in the life of the addict that he or she truly starts to participate in the same impaired mental processes of the addict. As "courtship goes awry" for the addict, the grief cycle for the loved one also becomes distorted. By definition, the addict replaces normal human relationships with sexual compulsiveness. Loved ones feel the loss, try to deny it, and become angry, feeling despair and sometimes hope. The co-addicts' efforts to restore the relationship are not only ineffective, they can intensify and deepen the addictive system for the addict. To compound the tragedy, co-addicts will make actions which are degrading, self-destructive, or even profound violations of their own values. Family members, as co-addicts, become part of the problem. Hence, the prefix "co."

Ruth Coe maintained that her son was innocent. Publicly, she was regarded as a mother who was attempting to protect her son. Her attempt to hire someone to kill the judge and prosecutor who sent her son to prison clarified for everyone her lack of reality about her son's actions. Co-addicts will go to extreme lengths to preserve the exterior world of the addict. By their actions they enter the insanity of their own interior co-addictive world.

The story of Beth illustrates well how the co-addict will distort reality in response to the addiction. Beth's parents were alcoholic. As a child she did everything possible to look good or be good. The violence and punishment were so great in her family, she went to any extent to avoid conflict. Her extra efforts at school, her extracurricular activities, and her jobs served many purposes. She was away from home as much as possible, she did not get into trouble, and she received attention for doing well. Although competent, Beth felt inadequate most of the time. She believed she had to prove herself over and over.

Men were a special problem. Beth was attractive but saw herself as homely. She did not trust the advances of men. Sexual experiences were disappointing since Beth always felt exploited—until she met Gene. Beth saw Gene as the ideal man for her. Besides being attractive, Gene also came from an alcoholic home. In fact, part of their initial attraction was that they agreed they would never do what their parents did. Beth felt secure that, even though Gene drank, he had been hurt as she was and would not become an alcoholic. Beth was also flattered by Gene's attention, given his involvement with a number of different women. When he broke off an engagement with another woman, she truly felt chosen. In short, Beth saw him as the perfect male.

Beth's first question about Gene's faithfulness to her came about three months after their marriage. Gene had lost his wedding band. Since they were short on money, they did not replace it. Gene's story about the loss of the ring was plausible, yet she was bothered by it. Her secret fear was that she might not be sufficiently attractive, competent, and interesting to keep a man.

Two events accentuated that fear. About a year after they were married, Beth saw Gene in a park with another woman. Upon confronting Gene with having an affair, she separated from him for three months. Ultimately, Gene convinced her that it was a meaningless mistake and that they should start over again. The second event occurred shortly after the birth of their second child. Beth discovered another affair about which she was intensely jealous. The combination of Gene's remorse and the burden of two little ones convinced Beth to make the best of it.

Gene was finally arrested for exhibitionism. He was not prosecuted, but it created quite a stir in the neighborhood. Beth was shocked and crushed, but this event was only the beginning. A neighbor friend who had heard about Gene came over. She asked Beth if she had trouble getting babysitters. In fact, Beth had begun to wonder if their two children had become monsters since all the regular sitters seemed to be "too busy." The neighbor suggested that she talk to the girls again and find out why they would not come. Beth coaxed the girls into admitting that Gene had, in fact, molested two of them on the way home. He had exposed himself to another while she was babysitting his children. Beth asked that they tell no one, that she would take care of it.

When confronted, Gene had a story for each instance, including the exposure; he said he went to the shower "not realizing the children and the sitter were around." She did not believe him but acted as if she did. Somehow she felt it was her fault for not meeting his sexual needs.

Beth became preoccupied with Gene's sexual obsessiveness. She only hired boy sitters. She would throw out his *Playboy* and *Penthouse* magazines. She watched him constantly to see if he was "rubbernecking" as attractive women went by. She became distant and cold. Her criticisms of Gene were harsh and judgmental. She often thought of leaving. She even thought of having affairs in retaliation.

In addition, Gene's drinking was becoming a problem. Beth found herself reacting to Gene in much the same way she had reacted to her parents. She became very active in the community, the children's schools, and had a part-time job. She found living with Gene easier when it was "as if two ships were passing in the night." The drinking was bothersome, but Gene's sexual involvements were terrifying.

The last straw came one day when Beth called an old friend she had not seen in a long while. She became instantly aware that something was wrong. Asking her friend to be candid, Beth was not prepared for her story. Amid sobs and hesitations, her friend reminded her of a party to which the three of them had gone. Beth was dropped off. Gene drove the friend home. He walked her to her apartment and invited himself in. He made advances. When she resisted, he forcibly raped her. The friend explained that she did not think anyone would believe her. She had allowed him in and even thought she might have been responsible since both of them had been drinking and flirting earlier at the party.

Beth was furious. Gene did not deny her friend's story. In fact, he told Beth that he felt really bad about the whole thing and knew it was because of the drinking. The timing was incredible since Gene's employer had just that day told Gene he had to go in for a diagnosis for alcoholism. Beth was dumbfounded. She knew that Gene had a problem with drinking—but the real problem was sex. Gene went to treatment partly out of his shame about the revelation of Beth's friend. During treatment, however, the program staff quickly helped Gene and Beth to realize there were two addictions present. Beth was obsessed with one and had been blind to the other.

Gene discovered in treatment that his sexual compulsivity did not start with his marriage. Gene had brought to the marriage a complete fusion of sex and relationship. His obsessiveness went back to grade school when he would sneak out regularly at night, climb a tree, and watch a neighbor lady undress. He also had been sexually abused, starting at the age of six by a babysitter. He even remembered a series of abusive events in his parochial high school with friends, teachers, and priests. One priest, in fact, regularly fondled Gene's genitals during confession while explaining how masturbation was a sin. He would say, "You know you are not supposed to use this," as Gene would become aroused. That event pictured for Gene what his youth was about—a double message about humiliation and excitement he never outgrew.

Like most addicts, Gene discovered that marriage did not change his compulsiveness. Within three months of marrying Beth he was involved with other women. He did love Beth, and he did not even like the women with whom he was involved. The woman Beth saw in the park was someone Gene really hated, but would have sex with. With the separation, Gene vowed never to be sexual again with anyone outside the marriage. His promises to Beth had the ring of sincerity rooted in his commitment to change. Yet, it was only a matter of time before he was involved again. As repeated efforts to stop failed and as his sexual behavior extended to exhibitionism, Gene's profound discouragement about himself increased. The presence of children simply added to the pain. Gene experienced what every addict who is also a parent experiences—to look at his children and wonder what they would think if they knew.

In treatment, Beth realized that her history with Gene revealed a consistent process in which she sacrificed her own identity—giving up a part of herself in order to stay in the relationship. This process included:

> disregarding her own intentions.
> overlooking behavior which hurt her deeply.
> covering up behavior which she despised.
> appearing cheerful when she was hurting.
> avoiding conflict to keep up appearances.

being disrespected repeatedly.
allowing her own standards to be compromised.
faulting herself for the family's problems.
believing she had no options.

Everything Beth did was absolutely similar to what she did to survive as a child in an alcoholic family.

Beth's loss of self also paralleled the loss Gene suffered. Gene's life had been taken over by addiction. Beth, too, was caught in a process beyond her control—a process in which her reactions made the situation worse. Beth truly was a co-addict.

The Co-addictive System

The co-addictive system parallels the process of the addictive system. Co-addiction starts with fundamental or "core" beliefs about one's self, relationships, needs, and sexuality. These beliefs generate impaired thinking which distorts reality and fosters co-addictive behavior. This is behavior by which the co-addict attempts to change the addict, but which in reality contributes to the addiction. Co-addictive behavior adds to the unmanageability of the family members' lives. When the unmanageable consequences confirm the core beliefs, the co-addictive system grows and perpetuates itself.

THE CO-ADDICTIVE SYSTEM

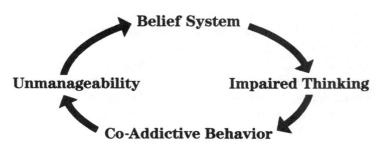

Belief System

Impaired Thinking

Co-Addictive Behavior

Unmanageability

Each part of the system reinforces the others.

The belief system again is key. Cultural and family messages affect what the child holds to be true. In many ways, the co-addict's core beliefs are the same as the addict's. Beth's belief about her basic undesirability limited her relationship possibilities. In order to survive and have her needs met, she felt she had to pretend that everything in the relationship was acceptable when it was not. The same sense of abandonment which addicts experience in their lives exists for co-addicts. A complete discussion of co-addicts' core beliefs appears later in this chapter. At this point the reader only needs to see the central role of the belief system.

Since the belief system filters the reality of the co-addict, impaired thinking results.

First, there is *denial*. At its most subtle, denial is dismissing your own intuitions. At its most blatant, it is overlooking what is right in front of you. Both Ruth Coe and Beth had clear indicators that there was a serious problem but chose not to see it. One incestuous father used to have an elaborate ritual of making a special bed for his daughters late at night. He would go get his daughters out of bed, take them to the extra bed, be sexual with them, and throw the sheets in the wash. During the eight years that this was a weekly occurrence, the mother never voiced any curiosity about where the extra sheets came from.

Denial is usually supported by extensive *rationalization*. Beth always had sound reasons to dismiss her feelings and reality. She even assured herself that if they were making love on a regular basis it must be all right. Sometimes the family member's logic just does not make sense to outsiders. Ruth Coe faced that with the jury who convicted her son. He was accused of using colored transparencies to make his car license plates appear as out-of-state plates. Her explanation was that he had used it to protect his personalized plates—which he no

longer had. Moreover, she thought it was so fashionable she
wanted him to do it for her car.

Grandiosity and *inadequacy* are flip sides of the same coin
for the family members. Because they feel their own "failings"
so deeply (inadequacy), they feel responsible for other people's
actions (grandiosity). For example, "If only I had been more
sexual, he would not have to do this." It is grandiose for the
wife to assume responsibility for her husband's sexuality. She
does so because she feels so inadequate. So it works with all
members of the family . . . "If only I had been a better child,
parent, brother, or sister . . . "

Perhaps the most damaging dynamics of the impaired thinking
are blame and judgment. The co-addict judges the addict as the
source of all of the family's problems. Blaming the addict
protects the co-addict from the vulnerability of telling the addict
about personal hurts and fears. There is absolute safety in blame.

In healthy relationships, intimacy becomes possible when
people accept the risk of rejection and reveal their internal
struggles. Such self-disclosure between partners:

—indicates trust.
—affirms the other person.
—takes responsibility for own actions and feelings.
—shares common problems.
—interrupts the addictive system.

Blame, however, builds barriers instead of intimacy because it:

—indicates distrust.
—lowers self-worth.
—builds defensiveness.
—denies personal responsibility.
—prevents efforts to work on common problems.
—intensifies the addictive system.

Blame, denial, secrecy, grandiosity, and rationalization together shield the co-addict's internal feelings of fear, hopelessness, and inadequacy. A person who is grieving the loss of the original relationship with the addict may refuse to accept reality, become angry and blaming or even start to bargain with the addict. The co-addict wishes to stave off the pain that admitting the loss would bring. Similarly, the co-addict distorts reality in order to preserve the relationship. Even the most self-righteous blame preserves the co-addict's connection because by preoccupation with the addict's problems the co-addict can remain involved.

Preoccupation with the addict's sexual behavior bridges the gap between impaired thinking and co-addictive behavior. The co-addict's obsession with whether the addict is acting out or not obscures the co-addict's self-awareness. The desperate concentration pushes loneliness, pain, and vulnerability aside.

Preoccupation with the addict's problems leads to *controlling behavior* on the part of the spouse, parent, or significant other. When Beth threw out her husband's magazines, she was acting like the spouse of the alcoholic who pours booze down the drain. Neither one is effective in controlling addiction. The family member's efforts to control are rooted in the grandiose thinking that they can do something about shaping up the addict. Overt efforts to control include watching the addict, demanding accountability for all time spent, not trusting the addict to act responsibly, and even setting traps for him. These efforts are intensified by self-righteous criticism, blame, and judgment. The family tries to prove that the addict is the bad person and needs to change. The addict receives the message. (There is no other conclusion, given the addict's core beliefs.)

The co-addict uses the sexual relationship between them as one of the chief methods to control the addict. Controlling sex comes from the co-addict's preoccupation with the sexual behavior of the addict. Sexual manipulations include:

—withdrawing sex as a punishment.
—having sex as a reward.
—threatening sex with others to create jealousy
in the addict.
—having sex with others to retaliate.
—acting or dressing sexy to gain attention.
—being sexual with the addict to prevent the addict
from being sexual with others.

In the short run, the co-addict can manipulate the sexual obsession of the addict. In the long run, the co-addict simply provides proof for the addict's belief that the most important need cannot be predictably met.

Enabling, in contrast to controlling, stems from denial and rationalization. Covering up for the addict, protecting him or her from consequences, and keeping silent about personal concerns are the behavioral ingredients of enabling. It involves a fundamental dishonesty which entails the insane denial of what one knows to be true. Beth often took the consequences for Gene. The paradox is that she could only do that by assuming she could change Gene.

Participation in secrecy clearly enables the addict's illness. When Beth asked the babysitters to not tell anyone, she too entered a double life. Beth was acting on two myths. The first was that all problems are to be solved within the family. The second was the conviction that she could control or stop the addiction. The efforts of the family members end up fueling or enabling the addiction, not stopping it. The veil of secrecy around the addictive behavior prevents outside feedback from restoring to the addict and family members a true grasp of reality. When Beth's neighbor confronted her, she was asking Beth to face up to a real problem, not bury it.

In fact, both of the co-addict behaviors, controlling and enabling, rest in the assumption that the co-addict has power over the addict. Paradoxically, co-addicts also fear that their efforts will not be enough to eliminate the addiction. When the addicts fail to change, co-addicts interpret that to mean they must try harder. However, since the addicts are in fact powerless, the co-addicts' efforts are doomed to failure. Yet co-addicts allow themselves to believe they have found the right solution. Hope alternates with despair in the the co-addicts' lives.

With the addict at the center of the co-addict's world, the co-addict's life becomes *unmanageable*. Co-addicts report all types of consequences:

—neglect of spiritual life
—loss of friendships
—unusual dreams
—changes in eating and sleeping patterns
—accidents, illnesses or injury due
  to the stress of addiction
—loss of time on the job
—decreased ability to work or function
—conflicts with value system or personal ethics
—suicide attempts or thoughts
—financial problems
—takeover of addict's duties and responsibilities
—overextension and overinvolvement in work
  or outside activities
—self-defeating or degrading behavior

The "Co-addict's Checklist" on pages 100 and 101 is provided to help spouses, family members, and others identify their co-addictive behaviors.

Once the family has entered the unmanageable double life of the addict, the whole family unit becomes progressively more *isolated*. Participation in the secrecy, enabling, controlling, grandiosity—all generate a collective complicity in the addiction. At a fundamental level, family members understand that and erect *external barriers* to public scrutiny. These barriers also reduce the chances for effective help.

The general family isolation amplifies the loneliness of each of the members. *Increasing distance between family members* becomes the norm in the family. Rather than admitting to a personal need, it is easier for an individual member to be critical of others. When there is a chance for real intimacy, it is evaded by silence or by fighting. Some families stay connected through their fights, but the individual members remain lonely. Because family members do not have *effective linkages* with each other or with outsiders, they make *ineffective responses* to crises. Problems often require everyone's cooperation to solve. Outside help can be necessary too. Problems which are not resolved—financial, work, parenting—simply add to the unmanageability and personal chaos.

Unmanageability causes family members to feel shameful about their family, although they are quick to defend it. In effect, they have a low concept of themselves as a family as well as individuals. Deteriorating family and personal pride validates the core beliefs of each family member who supports the addiction. To understand that connection more fully, one must see the role core beliefs play in the co-addict's world.

The Co-addict's Core Beliefs

When Joanne's daughter told her about the incest, she did not believe her. In fact, she berated her daughter for even talking like that about her father. Two years later when her daughter ran away Joanne learned the truth. She saw that she had enabled her husband's addiction to last two years longer. During treatment she realized that her denial and enabling originated in the whole family's low self-esteem. She wrote in her treatment autobiography:

> And I've come to find out that our whole family was
> sick and needed help. The help that I started to get for

The following are typical co-addictive traits. Simply check off the ones which apply to you. The more items you check, the more you will see a co-addictive pattern in your life. A further step is to record in a private

☐   concealing behavior of the addict

☐   protecting the addict from consequences of behavior

☐   denial of the obvious

☐   alibis, excuses, and justifications to others

☐   feelings of responsibility for addict's behavior

☐   self-righteous criticism and judgment of the addict

☐   efforts to confront the addict with his or her "problem"

☐   feelings of superiority to addict

☐   overlooking addict's behavior

☐   distrust of others outside the family because of addict

☐   rationalizing addict's behavior

☐   fantasizing and obsession about addict's problem

☐   belief that if addict changed, all problems would disappear

☐   efforts to threaten or exact promises from the addict

☐   strategies to control sexual activity of addict

☐   attempts to "catch" or trap the addict

☐   being sexual with the addict to prevent the addict from being sexual with others

☐   intense mood swings from high to low

☐   on-going list of resentments and disappointments

☐   feelings of depression and remorse

☐   loss of friendships

CHECKLIST

journal or notebook as many examples as you can remember for each item checked. The result will be a descriptive picture of your total co-addictive system.

- ☐ deterioration of family "pride"
- ☐ secret pacts with other family members
- ☐ feeling distant from other family members
- ☐ distrust of each other within the family
- ☐ loss of self-esteem or self-respect
- ☐ growing self-doubt and fear
- ☐ feeling unique
- ☐ neglect of spiritual pursuits including prayer or meditation
- ☐ unusual dreams
- ☐ changes in eating or sleeping patterns
- ☐ accidents, illnesses, or injury due to the stress of addiction
- ☐ loss of time on the job
- ☐ decreased ability to work or function
- ☐ suicide attempts or thoughts
- ☐ efforts to control family expenditures with increasing failure to do so
- ☐ increasing financial problems
- ☐ takeover of duties and responsibilities of addict in effort to keep family life "normal"
- ☐ overextension and overinvolvement in work or outside activities
- ☐ engaging in self defeating or degrading behavior

my husband and daughter ended up being for me too. And I've learned a lot and I've come a long way. Self-esteem seems to be very low in all of these families, including mine. I guess as a child I just wasn't given the love that I needed. I don't know if that reflects on my parents any. Maybe they just didn't know how to give it either. I think that's why incest remains in the family from generation to generation, and it's commonly called the family secret. No one talks about it, no one lets on. Parents don't want to admit that they might be bad parents or have something wrong with them.

Co-addicts operate with the belief, *I am basically a bad, unworthy person.* Because they share this belief with the addicts, they participate in the addictive system easily. Co-addicts grow up in families in which their self-worth is constantly in jeopardy. Feelings of inadequacy and failure parallel the addicts' sense of unworthiness. Not believing there are any options, co-addicts tolerate abusive, humiliating, and degrading behavior. Being with an addict furthers the myth of "unlovability."

Self-righteous disdain often masks the interior fears of the the co-addict. Also, aggressive and critical controlling behavior switches with compliant enabling roles. Co-addicts report that these switches can occur within moments of each other. Either position shares a martyrdom role in which the co-addict is being "victimized."

Joanne described how these roles worked in her family:

I have come to realize that I sometimes take the place of my daughter and she becomes the wife and mother. I start acting just like a little girl. No wonder incest occurred so easily. I have also come to realize that my husband sometimes expects me to act like his mother, okaying things he does and even telling him what to do and still he tells me that if I am ever like his mom he will leave me. Insane? You bet.

The beliefs and impaired thinking of the addict "fit" well with the controlling or enabling behavior of the co-addict. Reacting to judgment and criticism as deserved, addicts also use it to justify abusive and compulsive behavior. When co-addicts are submissive and compliant, addicts feel burdened, critical, and exploited. Being responsible for all the family's decision-making, for example, may make the addict into a "parent" for the co-addict as opposed to a partner. These feelings also serve as a rationale for addictive behavior.

Co-addicts add to their first belief a second: *No one would love me as I am.* Co-addicts in relationships reflect their basic distrust of other people. To be in a relationship engages the three co-addictive fears: that co-addicts would lose their identities in the relationship, that they would deny what they know is real, and that fulfilling their needs would have a price. To tell others the painful "secrets" would guarantee abandonment. To be honest with or vulnerable to the addict would sacrifice the safety of being self-righteous or compliant. Co-addicts, like the addicts, assume that they are responsible for all the pain in loved ones:

Joanne wrote about how she kept her distance:

> I have really built up an indifferent attitude toward my husband and by doing this I have somehow managed to put a wall of mistrust around me. This has kept me from experiencing the warmth of others. If someone hurt me I laughed rather than cried. I didn't want them to know I was in pain. I can't ever remember being held as a child even though I wanted to be. I still do. I would shirk off an arm that was put around me and wouldn't let anyone hold my hand for fear I would get too close to them. I remember the first time my counselor put her arm around me. I just broke down in tears that I had never had before and sank into her arms. I

needed somone to hold me and understand my pain.
I didn't have to be anyone special or anything for
her to care and because of that I am learning to care
and share my love. I can reach out to another and
tell them to understand more easily every day. I
wouldn't have done that six months ago even if I
felt like it. *Love doesn't have a price tag* and as I
experience the hope this program gives me and
accept myself I am becoming able to love others and
I am finding I have a lot to give back and trust seems
to be there too. I have reached out and learned that
not everyone goes away. Some reach back and we
get a lot of support from each other.

Co-addicts may go to extreme lengths to appear self-
sufficient. They appear unaffected by any problems and will
expend intense energy to conceal problems. In fact, co-addicts
will take on many extra responsibilities, being all things to all
people. They often seek relationships in which they dominate
or nurture because they can be intimate with minimum risk.
Just as co-addicts sometimes make addicts into "parents," co-
addicts will treat addicts as "another child in the family." This
self-sufficient exterior protects the secrets of the family and
precludes the co-addict from having to acknowledge his or her
personal needs. Also, the internal belief that the co-addict is
responsible for everything is acted out.

Joanne's overly responsible behavior was typical:

My husband used to bring me home his paycheck
every week. He was a very good husband. And I
took care of paying all the bills out of it. But he
wanted some spending money. I never could tell him
that there wasn't enough money to go around and I
didn't have enough to give him spending money, so
I gave him what he wanted and robbed Peter to pay

Paul and eventually Peter and Paul wanted to be
paid. And then I'd have to hide the bills. I would
even hide things that I bought for me. After all,
didn't his paycheck come totally to me? He could
have gone out and spent it on something else, but
he always brought it home to me. Somehow I should
have the power to make it stretch. I finally had to
admit that I had limitations. And the phone calls
from the collectors sure proved unmanageability. I
learned about that in part of the First Step, too. I
came to realize that I'm not responsible for my
husband and his actions. Many times I made excuses
for the things he said or did that I somehow didn't
agree with, and I felt others didn't agree with, either.
I'd try to explain away his reasoning. I've learned
that my first obligation is to manage my own life.
Let go of what I can't control and trust God to help
me. It's a daily thing and can only be done one day
at a time.

Addicts often rely on co-addicts to pick up the pieces—
especially as powerlessness and unmanageability increase.
However, addicts may start to be critical of co-addicts' efforts,
criticizing mistakes they've made while performing extra
chores. For instance, if the wife has taken over the family's
bookkeeping, her husband may fault her if the checkbook
doesn't balance. The criticism stems from the addicts feeling
progressively more useless and without a place in the co-addicts'
lives. The addicts feel unneeded especially when the co-addicts
are busy nurturing others, like children. The co-addicts' involvements serve as further justification for compulsiveness.

The next core belief also parallels the addict's belief: *My
needs are never going to be met if I have to depend upon others.*
The co-addict's desperate need for love and nurturing exceeds
any one person's ability to respond. The co-addict's high

expectations fit with other efforts to control the addict. When he or she is disappointed because the addict failed to meet the highest expectations, the co-addict's rage becomes internalized, resulting in despair, self-pity, and resentment. These down times alternate with periodic exhilaration and hope that things will change. Conniving manipulation and criticism are based on the assumption that if the addict were to meet the high standards, the co-addict's needs would be met. The addict becomes the source of the co-addict's self-worth and good feelings. The conviction that the co-addict will have to pay for love and care pervades all relationships. To be loved and cared for with no requirements goes beyond the co-addict's experience.

Joanne aptly described this process:

> My ability to respond to my needs and to the needs
> of others is really hard. Most of the time I simply
> react. I often try to be responsible for everyone and
> everything. When that happens it results in a lot of
> frustration and a lot of anger, even self-pity. I have
> had to realize that I am only responsible for me and
> my reactions and try real hard to quit controlling.
> At first I was trying to blame my husband or anyone
> else who was available for what was going on and
> what I was going through. I had to learn that I alone
> had to be responsible for my faults. I had to stop
> nagging, complaining, and criticizing. I had to stop
> being the manager, accuser, and judge, and I had to
> stop forcing issues. Forcing issues came easy and
> still does. It is hard to let go.

Martyrdom is a part of the co-addicts' systematic efforts to make themselves indispensable to the addicts. In exchange, the co-addicts expect the addicts to furnish proof of care and love. Failure to do so results in further efforts to reform or shape up the addicts or in self-righteous punishment and rejection. The co-addicts do not communicate personal needs, only disappointed expectations. Preoccupation with the addicts often results in the denial or tolerance of the addicts' behavior. Co-addicts "keep score" of what is owed in the relationship. The more co-addicts do for the addicts, the more they expect from them.

Addicts fail to perceive co-addicts' needs. Partially, their failure stems from the addictive preoccupation and sexualization of all needs. The co-addict's behavior, however, also obscures the issues in the relationship. The addict grows resentful of the expectations yet also feels a sense of failure for not meeting them—which no one person could do. Co-addictive judgments simply document what addicts already fear to be true. Yet, addicts remain confident co-addicts will not leave their relationship because of the co-addictive preoccupation. As long as they are still judging, they are still there.

The final core belief is the only one in which co-addicts differ substantially from addicts. Instead of seeing sex as the most important need, co-addicts often believe: *Sex is the most important sign of love*. As children, co-addicts confused sexual interest with care. They were just as lonely, but they learned quickly that they could gain attention, warmth, and care by acting cute and sexy. Also, the uglier someone feels, whether truly so or not, the more sexual he or she acts to gain the attention needed.

Sex also became a vehicle by which fundamental nurturing needs were met. If a child was sexually abused by someone important to him, that further confirmed the belief. Being sexually abused teaches the child that in order to have a relationship, one has to be sexual. Abuse victims grow up as adults who believe sex is the price to be paid for nurturing. If one of these children eventually marries a person whose major source of comfort is sex, their relationship relies on sexual intensity to carry it.

107

Therefore, co-addicts have the conviction that sexual attention affirms the whole person. Sex becomes one of the most tangible trade-offs for love. Therefore, co-addicts have a great fear of being unattractive and sexually inadequate. When the addicts are sexual with others, the co-addicts feel total personal rejection. Given the stakes, co-addicts have difficulty exploring or enjoying their own sexuality. Because of the repeated disappointments in sex as a way to meet relationship needs, they continue to distrust. Experiences where the co-addicts are exploited foster deep resentment and rage which further validate all the co-addictive core beliefs.

By being sexual in exchange for love, co-addicts may find themselves being sexual when they do not wish to be, or worse, participating in sexual behavior that is degrading or humiliating. Co-addicts may also dress or act seductively to get attention. Efforts to control the addict's sexual obsession include the use of sex to prevent the addict from being sexual with others. Sexual attitudes of the co-addicts may reflect their other external themes of self-sufficiency, indifference, self-righteousness, and martyrdom.

Addicts feel confused by the conflicting signals from the co-addicts about sex. Often addicts misinterpret the co-addicts' needs for relationships as sexual overtures. As a result, addicts totally fail to understand the exploited feeling of the co-addicts. The addicts feel ashamed when sexual feelings are not returned since that validates that their sexual intensity is bad. Also, addicts resent the co-addicts' efforts to control and judge their sexual behavior, all of which perpetuates their addiction system.

The Family Illness

The delicate balance of human ecology we call a family relies on the interdependency of its members. When issues around self-esteem, relationships, and needs are not resolved, the impact is felt throughout the entire web of relationships. When those issues evolve into addiction and co-addiction, the loving bonds become a prison. The entire family—maybe for generations—participates in thought and action.

Understandably, addiction of all kinds thrives in such an environment. Alcoholism and compulsive overeating are frequent partners in the sexual addiction dance. The husband justifies his sexual addiction because "she is always drunk." The wife who adds a hundred and fifty pounds as an expression of her rage or as a statement about sexuality is also doing something her husband cannot control. In a family with *multiple addictions,* the varieties of addiction and co-addiction simply reinforce one another. Each addiction may involve different behaviors, but shares a common addiction system.

When the family balance is upset by the addiction of one or more members, the task of renewal requires that each member—addict or co-addict, child or grandparent—take responsibility for his or her part. The shift of the energy from blaming others to ownership of personal action creates a new environment of trust. Taking responsibility starts with a thorough knowledge of one's own belief system. That is the goal of the next chapter.

THE WORLD OF THE

CORE BELIEF 1
SELF-IMAGE: I am basically a bad,
unworthy person.

Interior World

Co-addicts grow up in families in which their self-worth
is in constant jeopardy. Feelings of inadequacy and failure
parallel the addicts' sense of unworthiness. Not believing
there are any options, co-addicts tolerate abusive, humiliating, and degrading behavior. Co-addicts are obsessed with
sex since sex is the proof of love.

Exterior World

Self-righteous contempt often masks the co-addicts'
interior fears. Aggressive, critical, controlling behavior
switches with compliance and enabling. Either position
shares a martyrdom role in which the co-addict is being
"victimized."

The Addicts'
Response to
Co-addicts

Addicts are in a self-serving double bind in the relationship.
When co-addicts are critical and judgmental, addicts use
this to justify abusive, compulsive behavior. When
co-addicts are submissive and compliant, addicts feel
burdened, exploited, and critical. These feelings also serve
as a rationale for addictive behavior.

CO-ADDICT

CORE BELIEF 2
RELATIONSHIPS: No one would love me
as I am.

Interior World

Co-addicts in relationships reflect their basic distrust of others' love and care for them. To be in a relationship engages the three co-addictive fears: that co-addicts would lose their identities in the relationship; that they would be forced to deny what they know to be true; and that meeting their needs would have a price. To tell others the painful "secrets" would guarantee abandonment. To be honest with the addicts would sacrifice the safety of being self-righteous or compliant. Co-addicts, like addicts, assume that they are responsible for all the pain in loved ones.

Exterior World

Co-addicts go to extreme lengths to appear self-sufficient. They seem unaffected by any problems and will expend intense energy to conceal problems. In fact, they will take on many extra responsibilities, being all things to all people. In general, they often seek relationships in which they can dominate or nurture so they can be intimate with minimum risk. This self-sufficient exterior protects the family secrets. Also, the internal belief that the co-addicts are responsible for everything is acted out.

The Addicts'
Response to
Co-addicts

Addicts rely on co-addicts to pick up the pieces—especially as powerlessness and unmanageability increase. Yet, addicts may start to be critical of co-addicts' efforts when they assume extra responsibility. Internally, addicts start to feel progressively more useless and without places in the co-addicts' lives. Addicts feel unneeded especially when co-addicts are busy nurturing others such as children. The co-addicts' involvements serve as further justification for compulsiveness.

CORE BELIEF 3
**SELF-IMAGE: My needs are never going to be met
if I have to depend on others.**

Interior World

Co-addicts' desperate need for love and nurturing exceeds any one person's ability to respond. They make perfectionistic demands on all aspects of the addicts' behavior in a misdirected attempt to guarantee satisfaction of their needs. When they are disappointed by the addicts' failure to meet the impossible demands, rage becomes internalized resulting in despair, self-pity, and resentment. These down times alternate with periodic hope and exhilaration that things will change. Co-addicts' conniving manipulation and criticism are based on the assumption that if the addicts met the high standards, needs would be met. Addicts become the co-addicts' source of self-worth and good feelings. The conviction that the co-addicts will have to pay for love and care pervades all relationships. To be affirmed with no requirements goes beyond the co-addicts' experience.

Exterior World

Martyrdom accompanies the co-addicts' systematic efforts to make themselves indispensable. In exchange, co-addicts expect addicts to furnish proof of care and love. Failure to do so results in further efforts to reform the addicts or in self-righteous punishment and rejection. Co-addicts do not communicate personal need, only disappointment in unmet expectations. Preoccupation with addicts often results in the denial or tolerance of addicts' behavior. Co-addicts "keep score" of what is owed in the relationship. The more co-addicts do for the addicts, the more they expect in return.

**The Addicts'
Response to
Co-addicts**

Addicts fail to perceive co-addicts' needs. Partially, their failure stems from the addictive preoccupation and sexualization of all needs. The co-addicts' behavior, however, also obscures the issues in the relationship. Addicts grow resentful of the co-addicts' expectations, yet also feel a sense of failure for not meeting them—which no one person could do. Co-addictive judgments simply document what addicts already fear to be true. Yet, addicts remain assured co-addicts will not leave while they are co-addictively preoccupied—as long as they are still judging, they are still there.

CO-ADDICT *(Continued)*

CORE BELIEF 4
SEXUALITY: Sex is the most important
sign of love.

Interior World

Co-addicts believe sexual attention proves they are lovable. Sex becomes a trade-off for love. Therefore, co-addicts have a great fear of being unattractive and sexually inadequate. When addicts are sexual with others, co-addicts feel total personal rejection, adding to their sense of unlovability. Given the stakes, co-addicts have difficulty exploring or enjoying their own sexuality. Exploitive experiences foster deep resentment and rage which further validate all the co-addictive core beliefs.

Exterior World

Because sex is a trade-off for love, co-addicts may find themselves being sexual when they do not wish to be, or worse, participating in sexual behavior that is degrading and humiliating. Co-addicts may also dress or act seductively to get attention. Efforts to control the addicts' sexual obsession include the use of sex to manipulate addicts to prevent them from being sexual with others. Sexual attitudes of the co-addicts can continue the external themes of self-sufficiency, self-righteousness, and martyrdom.

The Addicts'
Response to
Co-addicts

Addicts feel confused by co-addicts' contradictory signals about sex. Often addicts misinterpret the co-addicts' need for relationship as sexual overtures and then totally fail to understand the co-addicts' feelings of being exploited. Addicts are ashamed when sexual feelings are not returned since that confirms that their sexual intensity is bad. Also, there are feelings of resentment about the co-addicts' efforts to control and judge the addicts' sexual behavior, all of which perpetuates the addiction cycle of the addicts.

5

The Belief System

The contradictions which develop between the affectionate experiences of a childhood and the dehumanized relationships of adulthood create insoluble conflicts for both sexes. These conflicts take different forms in women and men....Our society creates psychic war within the two sexes and so perpetuates the war between them.

Helen Block Lewis
*Psychic War in Men
and Women*

The image of the seductive siren so powerful that even the bravest of men would succumb to her charms is as old as the Greek Ulysses' trek around the Aegean Sea. Powerlessness before women is a long-standing theme in Western classical and current literature. Part of every man can identify with some of the cartoon stereotypes: Dagwood being outmaneuvered by Blondie; Charlie Brown laughed at derisively by Lucy and her friends; or Hagar the Horrible becoming Hagar the Helpless in front of his wife. As a theme male powerlessness is as much a symptom of the sexual ills of our culture as are the many examples of the exploitation of women. The male sexual addict most visibly manifests this for he believes he is powerless in front of women. This chapter focuses on how cultural beliefs support the dysfunctional core beliefs of the addict. The central sexual beliefs of our culture are prime ingredients to the addictive systems which destroy men and women and their co-addicts.

In the perceptive words of Helen Block Lewis, we live in an exploitative society which "injures the two sexes differently."[1] Lewis characterizes men as "expendable warriors" who in their dominant role of providers must relinquish the human bonding which nourishes every human soul. Women, "the inferior childbearers," according to Lewis, maintain their capacity to nurture but give up significant parts of self-determination. Men become economic symbols. Women become sex symbols. The quintessential expression of the transaction is prostitution, i.e., money for sex. Its most injurious form is rape. From an addiction perspective, cultural expectations contribute to the addiction for both men and women.

Lewis points to societies in which providing and relationship responsibilities are shared. Responsibility for sexual initiation is also mutual. Either man or woman can reach out for one another without fear. Sexuality becomes an open and loving expression of the affection bond. When both men and women feel powerless in the presence of the other, sexuality can become a diminishing experience. Combining these cultural perceptions with the core beliefs of the addict generates compulsivity of enormous power.

The Cultural Beliefs

Warren Farrell, author of *The Liberated Man,* suggests that we are socializing or training men to be minirapists and women to be minimasochists. We develop in men the psychological characteristics of a rapist, but within an acceptable structure. The key factor in this socialization is that men are given the responsibility to initiate relationships and women are trained to be overcome. Farrell writes:

What is the effect on women of men's role to do the overcoming? Men learn to protect themselves from the hurt of rejection by turning women into sex objects. It is easier to accept rejection by an object than by a human being. If we can turn women into objects and sex into a game, talking about how far we got and whether we scored, it helps us avoid looking at why we were rejected. It helps us gain the courage to try even harder the next time (as we would in fulfilling an athletic role...). Each time a woman does not share in the initiative of obtaining the type of sexual involvement she wants, she is contributing to the use of herself as a sex object. Each time a man gives a woman negative feedback when she takes the initiative, he is contributing to his own frustration, to his anger and contempt for women (as objects that need to be persuaded to enjoy themselves), and to his need to use a woman as a sex object to protect himself from the very vulnerability he is reinforcing. Many women complain about men not being in touch with their feelings. It is dysfunctional for a man to be in touch with his feelings if he is going to be opening himself up to experiencing the pain of rejection. It is even more dysfunctional if he has to recover from the rejection and try again.[2]

Let us use men as an example. We will focus on women addicts later in the chapter. If a man comes from a family in which he feels bad about himself, has little confidence women would want to be with him, and believes that sex is the one comfort he cannot do without, addiction can occur. Place that same man in a culture which makes women into sexual objects and addiction will thrive. The belief system, the impaired thinking, the preoccupation and obsession, and the ritualization are all enhanced by cultural perceptions. People overlook powerlessness because it is the nature of men "to be carried away." As long as we de-personalize sex, men do not have to be responsible.

Addicts often talk about the difficulty of recovery. They live in a culture in which a major part of advertising efforts portray sex as central to good life. Addicts already struggle with personal obsession. They have to struggle with cultural sexual obsession as well. If the male addict went to men friends to share how he wanted to stop having affairs or seeing prostitutes, his friends might well respond, "Why would you want to do that?" Part of the male image is the conquest of women. Another part of the image, which advertising people know, is that men are susceptible to sexual overtures. They are perceived as powerless when it comes to their sexual needs. They will do what they can "to get it" and the best man is the one who succeeds in doing just that.

Given the pervasive quality of these attitudes, they have a severe impact on the addicts' core beliefs. The following chart ("The Male Sexual Addict's Beliefs about Sex, Men, and Women," pages 120 and 121) summarizes common perceptions held by male sexual addicts. These perceptions result from the fusion of faulty core beliefs with dysfunctional cultural attitudes. The perceptions reflect the addicts' low self-worth and alienation and their basic confusion that sexual expression will relieve their personal pain. Also reflected are the conflicting cultural roles of men and women. Stated in its most extreme form of dysfunction: women decide whether men will have sex or not. Men control economic security.

For the addict, two themes emerge. The first is an overwhelming need for sexual contact. He experiences this need in an environment which bombards him with sexual titillation from newsstands, television, and sales campaigns which use sex to market products. The second is a profound hopelessness that his sexual needs will not be met by other people. Or if they are partially met, it will not be enough. Seduction, illicit behavior, and manipulation all become options and also add excitement to the addictive cycle. For some addicts the ultimate bind emerges when you believe you must have it, but no one will give it to you. That profound sense of powerlessness can escalate to the use of force and the victimization of others.

An important connection exists between powerlessness and victimization. Rollo May's already classic description of this relationship in *Power and Innocence* shows that in a very real sense it generates "madness." A person who feels powerless to influence his or her situation is extremely angry or mad. The more powerless the person feels, the more prone that person is to violence. May suggests that this is a helpful way to understand the anger characteristic of insanity or "madness."[3]

The levels of addiction described in chapter two provide a framework for understanding how the sexual addict's victimization of others is connected to his powerlessness. The more he believes he cannot influence his relationships with women, the more likely he is to perform Level Two and Three behaviors. Built on the premise that he is powerless, the addict's belief system becomes an elaborate structure of myths and delusions which he sees as reality, but in fact:

– diminish his self-worth.
– limit his possibilities in relationships.
– justify his victimization in terms of his needs.
– connect sexuality with survival.

The more dysfunctional the belief system, the higher the probability the addict's pattern of sexual compulsiveness will include the types of victimization found in Levels Two and Three.

All addicts must alter their fundamental "core beliefs" in order to recover. In that sense, they are no different from anyone confronted with personal problems. A good example is the pioneering publication, *The Structure of Magic* by Bandler and Grinder.[4] By examining the work of a number of successful therapists from different schools of thought, they distilled an important commonality: the most effective therapists were those who were able to help their clients broaden their perceptions of possible choices. In other words, most people have problems because they believe that there are only certain options—usually

THE MALE SEXUAL ADDICT'S BELIEFS

THE CORE BELIEFS

1. Self-image: I am basically a bad, unworthy person.

2. Relationships: No one would love me as I am.

3. Needs: My needs are never going to be met if I have to depend on others.

4. Sexuality: Sex is my most important need.

THE ADDICT'S SELF-PERCEPTION

I am not attractive, personally or physically. A woman would not choose me.

I will have to convince a woman to be with me.

My needs can only be met by luck or chance, careful strategizing, or the accumulation of money or power.

I need sex all the time, cannot get enough, and must not pass up any opportunities. I am the only one who needs sex this much.

ABOUT SEX, MEN, AND WOMEN

THE ADDICT'S PERCEPTION OF MEN

Other men are more attractive, more successful, and more likely to be chosen by women.

Men have to initiate relationships. Other men are more effective than I.

Men have external power in jobs and money but will give in on issues to keep women happy.

Men are more sexual than women and more free to enjoy it. They will take sex whenever they can get it and cannot be trusted around women.

THE ADDICT'S PERCEPTION OF WOMEN

Women choose men who are not like me. They prefer stronger, smarter, and more successful men.

Women can wait, pick and choose to accept relationship offers.

Women make decisions at home and in other areas. They are impressed by money, possessions, and security.

Women are less sexual than men and have to be coaxed into being sexual. Consequently they are responsible for moral behaviors and can use sex as a reward or punishment.

self defeating—open to them. The therapists must assist them in discovering new possibilities for themselves and others. Bandler and Grinder describe this task as basically a problem of language and conception, i.e., that there are more options than the patient believed there were.

Recovery means seeking new options, not only for the addict but for the entire family. Family members have faulty beliefs—both cultural and core beliefs—as part of their co-addiction. Together the whole family can take on the search for alternate ways of being together.

The Family Beliefs

The families filed into the room with an easiness that belied the fact that up until a few weeks ago they had never met. Children scampered. Adults chatted. For all intents and purposes, it could have been a church meeting. What these families shared, however, was sexual addiction. At least one member of each family was sexually compulsive to an extent where there were serious consequences and the family was referred to treatment.

In this treatment program, 70 percent of the families also had a chemically dependent member. Weight was also an issue for many. An inordinate number of wives, for example, had intestinal bypass surgery. The desperation and eagerness of the families to learn was reflected in the silence and quick attention the instructor received as she gathered them together.

The session started with the instructor explaining that in order to understand addiction, one needed to explore the belief system which gives it life. A belief system, she explained, contains an elaborate set of rules, values, and myths created by the family and culture and integrated into the family. All behavior and options are judged by these beliefs. A set of judgments about oneself (core beliefs) exists within that belief system, such as one's own sexuality. These judgments are key to the addictive process for all family members.

The instructor asked the families to divide into separate groups—adult men, adult women, adolescent boys, adolescent girls, and children. Each group received sheets of newsprint and marking pens. Each group appointed a secretary. The instructor then gave the assignment: what do you believe to be true about sex, power in the family, attractiveness, and money? The instructor asked the secretary to record these beliefs. The children were given a special instruction: what have you heard in your home about sex and what have you heard about money?

Within the men's group, the discussion started with a joke which was followed by nervous laughter—a signal of their anxiety. Slowly and then with greater enthusiasm the ideas started to flow onto the page:

Men have to initiate sex.
Men need it more than women.
Men have to pay for it.
Every man will try to get sex if he can.
Men are attracted to women; women aren't
    attracted to men.
Women don't need it—can do without sex.
Women have to be warmed up.
Women's sexual interest declines after marriage.
Women decide whether to have sex or not.
Women tease—keep you guessing.
Men will chase it—give up more to get it.
Women use it as a weapon/reward.
Men are responsible for earning money—women
    for spending it.

As the men talked, they realized that they had a number of beliefs in common. Women were seen as determining whether men will have what they "desperately" want—sex. They felt anger about women who "tease," about times women abandon men, and about the power women have over men. They commonly acknowledged how they fear they have "missed out" on sexual experience. They shared resentment about being only as good as their jobs or their income. As a group they believed they could easily be replaced—as long as the money kept coming.

Meanwhile, the women too compiled their list, as angry and untrusting as the men's list. Examples were·

Men treat women as objects.
Men have "their brains in their pants."
Men cannot be intimate or close—too macho!
Men are not trustworthy.
Men use their economic power—will not share it.
Women are "less" if they are honest about how
   sexual they feel.
Women suffer a double standard.
Women control with sex.
Women have to raise families "alone."
Women have to be "thin."

The tenor of the women's conversation also sounded angry— as well as punctuated with jokes to relieve the tension. One woman talked of how she hated being something to drain her husband's body so he could sleep. Others quietly nodded their heads in assent. Another added how she used sex to reward or affirm, but not to enjoy. She talked further about her deep self-doubts as to her sexual adequacy. Yet another talked of feeling "trapped"—being unable to leave her marriage. She constantly increased her tolerance to things she hated because she was afraid of being alone—and with no means of support.

The instructor then asked each group to have a representative read each list and explain the listings. The men started. As they finished, the instructor asked the women how they would feel if they believed each of the responses by the men were true—not necessarily that they were, but if they *believed* they were. The women acknowledged that they would feel full of rage.

They were particularly struck by the theme of how the men perceived women as in charge of their sexual relationships.

A spirited discussion started about what the men meant by teasing. The instructor intervened, pointing out that they needed to continue. When the women presented their list, the instructor asked the men for their reactions. Initially, the men kept silent. Then one man shared two reactions. The first was that he could see why the couples fought so much. The second was that it was helpful for him to realize that everybody was experiencing the same things.

Then the instructor asked the adolescents to present their lists. The lists were absolutely parallel to the adults. Teenage boys talked about the paralyzing fear of rejection and the pressure to impress. Girls talked of the helplessness of waiting to be picked and of the efforts to gain attention without being obvious.

Next the instructor turned to the children and had them share what they had heard about these issues in their homes. The halting presentation of the younger children provided a painful perspective for everyone. Phrases like "you were a whore" (dad to mom) or "you're not old enough to know about that" (parent to child) brought glistening tears to parents' eyes. The overwhelming expression of sadness and loneliness was incredibly poignant as the adults recognized that what their own children were experiencing now was but an echo of their own early years.

The instructor asked the parents to share with the group memories they had of their own childhood. One mother spoke of how frightened she was when her dad was sexual with her when she was twelve and how she thought his attraction for her was her fault. A father spoke about how harshly he was disciplined for masturbating. Another shared how as a kid he believed his parents were not sexual and that only he had those feelings—which were bad to have. He felt he had to pretend he was not sexual in order to be in his family. A woman talked of how from early in life she was aware that being sexual was a way for her to have her needs met. Simply put, sex was the price one paid.

The instructor then elaborated on the emerging concept that beliefs about sexuality are often recreated with each generation. When negative messages about sexuality join with distorted cultural expectations of men and women, intimacy becomes warped and communications become limited. In fact, the secrecy and shame connected with sexual behavior make it more difficult to get accurate information to dispel myths which might be hurtful. Here again is an environment in which sexual addiction can thrive.

The instructor used the example of the shared belief that "men were not trustworthy" when it came to sex. For the addict, the belief that men in general are not trustworthy fosters impaired thinking like, "I am only doing what everyone else is." Essentially, the belief justifies his obsession. For the co-addict who sees her husband as another "untrustworthy" man, she concludes that she has to go to some extraordinary effort to control his behavior. Her impaired thinking tells her that she is responsible for what he does. She becomes preoccupied with the addict's behavior.

The instructor suggested that an alternative exists for both of them. Understanding that both men and women are fundamentally intensely sexual alters the view of the world of the addict and co-addict alike. Each has to take responsibility for his or her own sexual feelings. Addicts no longer need to feel compelled to insane behavior in order to meet their needs. Co-addicts can focus their energy on developing their own sexuality as opposed to being obsessed with the addicts'. Sharing sexual initiative as well as economic opportunity can displace feelings of jeopardy and exploitation. When both addicts and co-addicts can accept their sexuality as an exciting and rich part of relationships, old myths are dispelled which equate sexual feelings with being bad. By challenging beliefs and cultural expectations, family members can find a path out of addiction.

With that as her final point, the instructor brought the evening to a close. They all made a large circle in which they shared reflections about what they had learned that evening. As the group broke up, there was much joking and teasing as the families said good-bye.

Treatment programs for sexual addiction offer educational workshops for the addicts and their families, like the one just described, to help families understand the various facets of beliefs and family life which are part of the addiction. In fact, many programs use a combination of education and therapy to dismantle those operational beliefs which support the addiction, as well as supply new tools and options. By far the toughest task that therapists face when working with families is helping all the members of the family acknowledge their own faulty beliefs. Each member turns family and cultural beliefs into statements about who he or she is. "A bad man is oversexed" becomes "I am a bad man because of my sexual feelings." These self-judgments form the basic elements of a self-concept. They are the "core beliefs."

The Core Beliefs

In the movie, *Looking for Mr. Goodbar,* Diane Keaton ably plays Theresa, a young woman who entered the double life of the sexual addict. In her external world she was known as a compassionate and generous teacher of deaf children. She also had a secret life dominated by compulsive sex. Starting with an affair with her college professor, she initiated a series of exploitive and abusive relationships. These progressed to one-night stands and anonymous sex, including ritualistic cruising at bars. The movie ends with Theresa being killed by a sexual partner she had known only a few hours.

The brutality of the ending underlined the movie's powerful statement about the despair of the addict. The scenes of her work as a teacher served as the perfect counterpoint to the underlying drama of her life—in fact, capturing the duality of which addicts often speak. The story of Theresa helps to illustrate the connections between family, cultural, and core beliefs. Since Theresa is a woman addict, the cultural expectations are reversed, revealing the belief dynamics more clearly. In fact, Theresa's experience points out the role beliefs play in the whole addictive system.

Theresa comes from a rigid, Catholic family with proscriptive attitudes about sexuality. For example, at one point in the movie, Theresa's encounter with a nun on the street reminds her of the negative messages of her upbringing. Theresa is not alone in her family in struggling with compulsive sexual behavior or the proscriptive rules of the family. Her sister is constantly at odds with her parents. The sister becomes pregnant and is unable to determine who the father is. She agrees to marry a man she has known for four hours. Their marriage has a steady diet of group sex and porno movies. Theresa is repelled and attracted at the same time.

With a dominating alcoholic father, spontaneity and intimacy were extremely limited in Theresa's family. Worse, Theresa had a dramatic bout with polio at age eleven. While there was some physical deformity, the emotional scars were deeper. Her disfigured back became a symbol throughout the movie of her feelings of being unacceptable and unworthy as a person, i.e., her core beliefs.

Unworthiness as a person was the cornerstone of Theresa's belief system. She rejected men who initiated sincere relationships because of her fear and distrust. She opted instead for a free-wheeling sexuality which precluded lasting relationships. Sexual obsession took over her life. The title, *Looking for Mr. Goodbar,* really referred to a search for intimacy and nurturing. Theresa's core beliefs precluded normal relationship possibilities and held sexuality as the only trustable human exchange with one exception: Theresa trusted the deaf kids because they needed her. In that sense her story parallels so many addicts who are in helping professions—physicians, ministers, teachers, therapists, nurses, and social workers. One way these people can trust relationships in their external world is when they are clearly needed.

Impaired thinking for Theresa stemmed from her belief system. For example, she complained to some of her sex partners about her resentment of men who tried to pay her for sex. Her anger betrayed how removed she was from the reality of how degrading her sexual experiences were. Her beliefs that she was not worthwhile and that sex would meet her needs obscured reality, including her eroding sense of self-respect.

Theresa, as all addicts, made attempts to stop her compulsive addictive cycle. She spoke of her "last night" of cruising in an effort to stop, which failed. The futility of her efforts were most poignant in a conversation Theresa had with a bartender. She invited him to have a drink with her. He declined, saying that for him even one drink was too many. Her poignant reply was, "Yeah, I have that trouble with men."

As her addition progressed, Theresa became more and more isolated. Like so many addicts, she refused to even sleep with a sex partner after being sexual. The ever-present belief system did not allow for any relationship connection beyond sex. In Theresa's mind, if she let someone sleep with her, he would discover her basic unworthiness and reject her.

The unmanageability of her life increased. Sexual bingeing and heavy drug use caused her to oversleep and come late to school, creating a serious breach with her students, the one group of people to whom she was still close. Her unmanageability and despair confirmed what she believed to be "truths" about her own unworthiness and the undependability of others.

The fundamental paradox of the movie is that the addiction would have been less obvious if the central figure had been a man. By some cultural standards Theresa's behavior would have been less obviously deviant for a man. Part of the movie's success in conveying its theme lies in making the pain of addiction more evident by casting a woman in the role of the addict.

Theresa, as a character, creates a special glimpse into the impact that cultural expectations have on women addicts. The image of the good woman as the guardian of morality who "needs to be overcome" by the right words, the right moment, or the right mood in order to respond sexually presents an immense contrast to the sexually compulsive woman. While cultural beliefs tend to support a male addict's obsession, they contribute to the shame of women addicts who measure themselves by the same social standards. They add to their shame when they feel they must be the "only" woman who acts this way—and it is that sense of uniqueness which is central to the secret world of any addict. Their loneliness represents the special burdens our culture places on women. That Theresa found herself at odds with the cultural expectations of some of her partners who expected to pay her was in fact part of the problem.

All addicts and co-addicts, both men and women, face the same task in recovery: understanding their belief systems and finding alternatives. Each person must unravel the contributions of culture and family to his or her core beliefs. To disrupt the addictive system, each person must enter a process which replaces faulty beliefs with healthy ones. Such a process needs to parallel the life-giving dynamics of a healthy family and culture. Therefore, the recovery process must be one which:

- builds relationships.
- separates the behavior from the person.
- establishes clear guidelines for behavior.
- promotes learning from mistakes.
- relieves shame about past behavior.
- allows for amends to be made.
- supplies on-going support and affirmation.
- creates a positive sense of self.
- acknowledges the human need for help and nurturing for both men and women.
- is a method for checking reality.
- is an on-going exercise in the development of trust.
- provides new options for behavior in relationships.
- accepts all family members with their strengths and weaknesses

For close to fifty years, members of Alcoholics Anonymous have lived such a process using the Twelve Steps. Starting with the First Step, the Program asks its members to have a realistic appraisal of their situation, to admit or acknowledge that they are part of something that is not only destructive but stronger than they are. It asks them to have faith and trust in the other members of the fellowship and in a power greater than themselves. In a committed community, addicts can start anew in the full knowledge that there is help. Part of their exploring new options requires a candid statement about what they have done to others. With the human acceptance of that admission, they can then make amends. To recover, addicts accept an invitation to live a discipline, a collected wisdom, a way of life—the Twelve Steps. There is only one on-going requirement—that they be willing to pass the principles of the Program on to others. For in their helping others, they recycle the new learnings, the affirmations, and the human contact. What had been a destructive cycle of illness becomes a life-generating cycle of health. The Twelve Steps as a process for developing new beliefs about oneself is the focus of the next chapter.

6

Twelve Steps to Recovery

Harold C. Lyon, Jr., the former director of federal education programs for gifted children, was sentenced yesterday to nine months in jail despite his pleas to a Virginia judge that he committed three sex-related misdemeanors because he suffers from a mental illness that caused him to be "addicted to sexual gratification."

> Washington Post
> April 28, 1982

We admitted that we were powerless over our sexual addiction—that our lives had become unmanageable.

> The First Step

Harold C. Lyon, Jr., had much to lose. He had a wife, seven children ranging in age from eighteen to twenty-seven, and a $50,000-a-year government post. A West Point graduate and former Army officer, his career as a nationally recognized educator grew with the publication of three books on sexual liberation and self-awareness—all of which came to an abrupt halt when he was arrested by Arlington detectives on charges of pimping and prostitution. Specifically, he attempted to recruit customers on behalf of the wife of a former State Department official. The newspaper account of his own words reveals his pain:

> "My career is totally destroyed; my reputation as a psychologist and educator are ruined." Lyon clenched his fingers as he stood

133

before the judge and apologized for "promoting a life style I know now is a sickness. Money was never my motivation. I would have paid to do what I did and I did pay a lot of money," he said, thanking the detectives who arrested him for "stopping me before my life went further down the drain, if possible."[1]

Further testimony of the impact of the sexual addiction came from Edith Lyon, his wife, who spoke of the pain she had at not being able to "see any way Hal's behavior was going to change."

The Lyon family recognized the obvious parallels between sexual compulsiveness and addiction to alcohol. Some sexually addicted families, however, went a step further. They started to use the proven principles of the Twelve Steps of Alcoholics Anonymous as a way to change their lives.

Though the Twelve Steps were developed by and for alcoholics, it was only a matter of time before they were utilized as a path for those who had other compulsive disorders, and other Twelve Step groups formed: Gamblers Anonymous, Overeaters Anonymous, and Emotions Anonymous. That it has taken so long for a program to emerge for the sexually compulsive is not surprising, given the complexity and intensity of the issues involved—not to mention the shame. Just now a network of groups is emerging across the country which uses the Twelve Steps as the basis for recovery from sexual addiction.

As early as 1975, a number of groups started independently in places like California, Massachusetts, and Minnesota. People who were familiar with the Twelve Steps and Twelve Traditions of Alcoholics Anonymous generated many groups. However, members of other Twelve Step Programs such as Overeaters Anonymous also started groups for sexual addiction. While the compulsive behavior may have differed, all shared the common reality of the sexually addictive system and its destructive cycle. The names varied considerably (Sexual Addicts Anonymous,

Loveaholics Anonymous, Sexaholics Anonymous, Sexual Abuse Anonymous). So did the groups vary in how they worked and held their meetings. Yet, they shared a common Program—the Twelve Steps.

Using this Program, families who have felt the same level of desperation as the Lyon family have been able to turn their lives around. The question remains as to how these Steps can help. The goal of this chapter is to show just that—how the Twelve Steps can work for sexual addicts and co-addicts.

Defining sexual addiction as a "pathological relationship to a mood-altering experience" becomes critical to understanding the impact of the Twelve Steps. Chapter one described how the sexual addict's obsession replaced all meaningful relationships in the addict's life. Like the alcoholic, the sexual addict's secret life became more important than all that the addict valued, including family, friends, and work. The addiction system, that is, beliefs, impaired thinking, compulsive behavior, and unmanageability—creates its own momentum which isolates the addict further and further. Chapter two specified the wide range of compulsive behaviors experienced by addicts which contribute to the addicts' alienation. Following that, chapters three and four showed how the addict's family contributes to and reinforces the addiction. Family members participate in the illness, intensifying the relationship problems. Rooted in the family experience, four core beliefs are central to the deterioration of relationships for both addicts and co-addicts. To summarize, these faulty core beliefs are:

1. I am basically a bad, unworthy person.
2. No one would love me as I am.
3. My needs are never going to be met if I have to depend on others.
4. Sex is my most important need (addicts), or sex is the most important sign of love (co-addicts).

The Twelve Steps of Alcoholics Anonymous

1. We admitted we were powerless over alcohol—that our lives had become unmanageable.
2. Came to believe that a Power greater than ourselves could restore us to sanity.
3. Made a decision to turn our will and our lives over to the care of God, *as we understood Him.*
4. Made a searching and fearless moral inventory of ourselves.
5. Admitted to God, to ourselves, and to another human being the exact nature of our wrongs.
6. Were entirely ready to have God remove all these defects of character.
7. Humbly asked Him to remove our shortcomings.
8. Made a list of all persons we had harmed, and became willing to make amends to them all.
9. Made direct amends to such people wherever possible, except when to do so would injure them or others.
10. Continued to take personal inventory and when we were wrong, promptly admitted it.
11. Sought through prayer and meditation to improve our conscious contact with God, *as we understood Him,* praying only for knowledge of His will for us and the power to carry that out.
12. Having had a spiritual awakening as the result of these steps, we tried to carry this message to alcoholics, and to practice these principles in all our affairs.

The Twelve Steps reprinted for adaptation by permission of AA World Services, Inc. Copyright 1939.

The Twelve Steps of Alcoholics Anonymous
Adapted for Sexual Addicts

1. We admitted we were powerless over our sexual addiction—that our lives had become unmanageable.
2. Came to believe that a Power greater than ourselves could restore us to sanity.
3. Made a decision to turn our will and our lives over to the care of God as we understood Him.
4. Made a searching and fearless moral inventory of ourselves.
5. Admitted to God, to ourselves, and to another human being the exact nature of our wrongs.
6. Were entirely ready to have God remove all these defects of character.
7. Humbly asked Him to remove our shortcomings.
8. Made a list of all persons we had harmed, and became willing to make amends to them all.
9. Made direct amends to such people wherever possible, except when to do so would injure them or others.
10. Continued to take personal inventory and when we were wrong promptly admitted it.
11. Sought through prayer and meditation to improve our conscious contact with God as we understood Him, praying only for knowledge of His will for us and the power to carry that out.
12. Having had a spiritual awakening as the result of these steps, we tried to carry this message to others and to practice these principles in all our affairs.

Cultural beliefs support these core beliefs, creating a belief system integral to the addiction.

The Twelve Steps can fundamentally interrupt and alter the addictive system. The Steps can restore the capacity for meaningful relationships by developing in addicts and co-addicts new beliefs to replace dysfunctional or faulty beliefs.

Recovering persons who use the Twelve Steps can say to themselves:

1. I am a worthwhile person deserving of pride.
2. I am loved and accepted by people who know me as I am.
3. My needs can be met by others if I let them know what I need.
4. Sex is but one expression of my need and care for others.

Each of the Twelve Steps contributes to the new beliefs. Some Steps, however, are more key to some core beliefs than others. Without losing sight of the interdependency of each Step in the Twelve Step Program, the role of key Steps in the change of each core belief can be shown. By examining each core belief separately, the Twelve Step process emerges as a clear path for addicts and co-addicts to have healthy relationships. It will be helpful to refer to the Steps listed on page 137 as you read on.

Core Belief Number One: I am basically a bad, unworthy person.

This belief expresses the self-concept of addicts and co-addicts. A positive sense of self precedes any possibility of closeness or intimacy. Without that fundamental acceptance of self, nurturing and intimacy can be closed out. Addicts who regard themselves as "unworthy" survive in a secret world in which obsession blocks pain and loneliness and in which they are accountable to no one. Only the addicts know the whole truth. Each effort to quit which fails adds to the addicts' sense of hopelessness. By keeping their obsession a secret, the addicts, as well as family members, maintain an illusionary sense of control and responsibility.

With the First Step, addicts and co-addicts admit their powerlessness and unmanageability. As the admission removes the veil of secrecy, they find that they share a common problem with others. They realize that their addiction—a potent combination of cultural, family, and personal belief systems—was much more powerful than they were. Their isolation guaranteed the failure of their efforts to control. Instead of secrecy and self-control, the addict or co-addict must admit to others the need for help and receive it.

It helps when the admission of powerlessness occurs in the presence of others who have shared the same problem. The admission is less frightening. Being surrounded by recovering people reinforces honesty. Also, their insight helps the addicts with the greatest realization in terms of the first core belief—that they are not bad persons. Rather, they were part of an illness that was destroying their lives.

By declaring the unmanageability of their lives, addicts and co-addicts are forced to recognize the ways they were destroying themselves and others. The First Step starts addicts and co-addicts on the path to reclaiming reality. Fully acknowledging the consequences of the addiction encourages them to commit to a Program which can arrest the illness.

Steps Two and Three ask addicts and co-addicts to make an act of faith that they can recover with the help of a Higher Power. Essentially these are spiritual Steps, yet they do not prescribe a religion. Rather, they invite addicts to stop and reflect about what gives their lives meaning and purpose. This reflective process serves as an antidote to feelings of unworthiness. To establish a relationship with God is the first bridge to trusting relationships with others. Ernest Becker put it most succinctly in his Pulitzer Prize-winning book, *The Denial of Death:*

> Perversion has been called a "private religion"—and that it really is, but it testifies to fear and trembling and not to faith. It is an idiosyncratic symbolic protest of control and safety by those who can rely on nothing—neither their own powers nor the shared cultural map for interpersonal action.[2]

The "private religion" of the secret world must give way to Steps Two and Three. Addicts and co-addicts discover that they are not alone, that they are not abandoned and therefore not bad and unworthy as they learn to trust a Higher Power and the fellowship.

Steps One, Two, and Three combine within the addict or co-addict to internalize a new belief: *I am a worthwhile person deserving of pride.* A new sense of pride is born. The power of the secret world is broken. Identity and integrity return. Since there is no longer a need to hide, addicts can become open to each other in the fellowship and accessible to others outside the Twelve Step community.

Core Belief Number Two: No one would love me as I am.

When addicts or co-addicts conclude that they are basically bad persons and thus do not love themselves, they add the parallel belief that no one else would love them either. Given this belief, the only path for them is to project an unreal image which protects the secrets of the addiction. Addicts and co-addicts live with constant tension, fearing the truth will be discovered and made public. Rejection and abandonment would follow.

Step Four asks for a moral inventory during which addicts and family members must be brutally honest with themselves.

This inventory includes strengths as well as weaknesses. An honest appraisal of strengths helps dismantle the basic convictions about being unworthy and unlovable. Assessing weaknesses helps addicts and co-addicts focus on changes they can make, thereby adding hope. Analyzing strengths and weaknesses together continues the Twelve Step theme of reclaiming reality about behavior, beliefs, and impaired thinking.

Step Five requires the sharing of the Fourth Step inventory with another person. This Step, more than any other, challenges the addicts' and co-addicts' beliefs that if someone really knew everything about them, they would be rejected. In the unconditional acceptance of another human being, a great release of pain often occurs. By being sorry for what they have done, addicts experience reconciliation and forgiveness. Because of the spiritual qualities of that experience, clergy are often sought to hear a Fifth Step.

Later in the Program, Steps Eight and Nine demand that addicts make a list of people they have harmed and make amends where possible. Going further than the forgiveness in Step Five, the Twelve Step Program teaches that addicts and co-addicts can make up for what they have done. They need not feel guilt and shame forever. Amends-making gives them the opportunity for dignity. They learn that when they make a mistake, they don't need to retreat into the secret world. In most cases, people will accept their efforts to right the wrongs they have done.

Steps Four, Five, Eight, and Nine help addicts and co-addicts tap into their own sources of renewal. They find that they will not be abandoned, as so many of them were in their families when they were children. Instead, they come to a new conclusion about themselves: *I am loved and accepted by people who know me as I am.* Their belief allows them to take responsibility for their behavior and their behavior becomes more congruent with their values. They can accept their mistakes, make amends, and receive forgiveness. Addicts and co-addicts can become responsive and responsible members of the human community.

Core Belief Number Three: My needs are never going to be met if I have to depend upon others.

Where the first two core beliefs dealt with self-acceptance and intimacy, the third core belief deals with dependency. Addicts and co-addicts distrust other people—believing themselves unworthy and unlovable. Therefore they conclude that they cannot depend on others. The addict asks, Who would meet the needs of someone unlovable and unworthy? Who will care, listen, sympathize, and nurture? Who will take over, be concerned, act on my behalf, give advice, or share their lives? Who will help me when I am lonely, hurting, or desperate? Everyone has those needs and feelings. But, the deprivation in the lives of addicts and co-addicts leaves them convinced those basic human gifts from healthy relationships will never be given to them. This belief leaves addicts and co-addicts rageful, manipulative, and secretive.

When they admit their need by joining a Twelve Step Program, addicts and their family members have their first experience in the care of the fellowship. The Program has no conditions or restrictions. Addicts and their families receive affirmation simply through admitting their needs. The care they experience provides a basic experience which allows addicts and co-addicts to trust a Higher Power and the human community to supply the care they need and to discard the old self-destructive behaviors they had used to feel better. When addicts and co-addicts depended on their sexual "connections," they found their lives empty and still unsatisfied. Depending on others does bring the fundamental affirmation of themselves as persons. Almost like children, both the addicts and co-addicts have to be taught (or to relearn) how to let others know about their needs. As they learn to ask, they discover a new belief: *My needs can be met by others if I let them know what I need.*

Steps Six and Seven demand from addicts and co-addicts a complete surrender to their dependency needs. Continuing the spiritual theme of the Twelve Step Program, these Steps ask addicts to totally rely on their Higher Power for their recovery. What a challenge for people who lived so many years convinced that they were the only ones who could be trusted to take care of themselves! By asking God and others to meet their needs— thereby giving up control—addicts and co-addicts see a new way to have their needs met. They don't need addiction to deal with anxiety or pain. To be dependent on God and others is an acceptable and preferable way to live.

Addicts and co-addicts fear that they will be let down if they rely on others. With the Program they learn that they can be angry when disappointed, which invites further human connection. In the past, they would have responded with an internalized rage, which kept others out, and which admitted no need. Even when others occasionally disappoint them, addicts and co-addicts must continue to acknowledge those essential needs— especially to their Higher Power.

Core Belief Number Four: Sex is my most important need.

Through the Twelve Steps, addicts and co-addicts learn the power the addiction has had in their lives. They discover they do not need the addiction to survive because what they really wanted could be found in the support of others. They start to live new lives with focuses on healthy human relationships as opposed to sex. They do need the Twelve Step Program consistently, however, because of the addiction's power. The conviction that the old obsessions, rituals, and behaviors will bring peace dies hard—especially under stress. Only by living the Program daily and experiencing other people's care continuously does that belief diminish.

The Twelve Steps are an on-going discipline. Steps Ten and Eleven simply make explicit that these Steps are a Program that the addict or co-addict lives daily. Step Ten urges them to continue to take personal inventory and when wrong, to promptly admit it. This basic honesty keeps the addict or co-addict rooted in reality and connected in relationships. Step Eleven asks addicts and co-addicts to improve their conscious contact with God through prayer and meditation. The openness to acknowledging human failings, as opposed to concealing them, goes along with a consistent effort to maintain spiritual openness.

In the early days of Alcoholics Anonymous, the Twelfth Step was the one that finally made the Program work. Step Twelve requires that addicts carry the message to other addicts as part of their spiritual awakening. They simply pass on what they have received in terms of care and support. Addicts and co-addicts learn that by assisting someone else, all of their learnings are recycled. The Twelfth Step is a measure of how far they have come as well as a reminder of how potent their addiction is.

Addicts and co-addicts find what their obsession could never satisfy: a deep and personal sense of self-worth and value. They can be affirmed and loved, as well as loving and affirming. A rewarding and varied sexual experience within the context of a significant relationship adds nurturing to one's life. Living the Program assures that sexual obsession does not direct one's life. So addicts and co-addicts come to a new belief: *Sex is but one expression of my need and care for others.*

Altering the core beliefs is not easy. The Twelve Steps require a rigorous honesty and a commitment to change. For a summary of the key Steps and Program principles as they affect the core

beliefs, see the following pages, ''The Twelve Steps and Changing Beliefs.''

To borrow from the ''Big Book'' of Alcoholics Anonymous,
''Some of us have tried to hold on to our old ideas and the
result was nil until we let go absolutely.'' Letting go begins
right at the start of the Program.

Starting the Program

When Dan's therapist told him that he was sexually addicted,
he was outraged! He thought his therapist was exaggerating.
Dan was certain his real problem was depression. He was simply
down all the time and he wanted to be happier. True, his life
had left a trail of broken relationships and he had some sexual
problems, but that was because he was so down all the time.
Yet his therapist had been extremely helpful on a number of
issues, so to keep him happy Dan agreed to attend a couple of
meetings of a group which used the Twelve Steps for sexual
compulsivity.

At this first meeting, the group asked that he attend at least
six times. Dan said that he would in order not to make a scene.
Inside, he was convinced that he did not need to be there. As
he listened, he became even more convinced since some of the
members were struggling with sexual compulsions that were
alien and even foreign to anything Dan had ever thought about
doing.

Dan set a goal of three meetings—enough to fulfill his
therapeutic assignment without prolonging the agony. During
his third meeting, one of the members talked of the notion that
''horniness equals loneliness.'' Dan listened intently as the man
talked of how he had learned to identify those times when he
was searching for a woman to take care of his anger and pain.
Dan knew exactly the type of panic and desperation that was

THE TWELVE STEPS

OLD CORE BELIEFS	PROGRAM PROVISIONS FOR BOTH ADDICTS AND CO-ADDICTS
1. I am basically a bad, unworthy person.	The Program provides the understanding that each member is basically a good person. All learn to separate themselves as individuals from their addiction which, as a powerful illness, is destroying their lives. By admitting the addiction's power, hope emerges from connecting with others and with a Higher Power.
2. No one would love me as I am.	The fellowship of the Program surrounds participants with people who have suffered in the same way. They no longer feel unique. They trust and are trusted with personal secrets. They have the opportunity to assess their strengths and weaknesses, as well as to take stock of their own values and behavior. Their new vulnerability allows them the hope of depending on others outside the Program. They rediscover the fundamental human processes for restoring relationships through amends and forgiveness.

AND CHANGING BELIEFS

KEY STEPS*	NEW BELIEFS	INTEGRATED WORLD
1,2,3	**I am a worthwhile person deserving of pride.**	Addicts and co-addicts have a new sense of pride. Power of the secret world is broken. Identity and integrity return. They no longer need to hide and can become open to each other and to others.
4,5,8,9	**I am loved and accepted by people who know me as I am.**	Addicts and co-addicts develop a realistic sense of their strengths and weaknesses, of their personal self-worth, and of the limits to their impact on others. They take a new responsibility for their behavior and their behavior becomes more congruent with their values. They learn that mistakes can be accepted, amends made, and forgiveness received. Addicts and co-addicts can become responsive and responsible members of the human community.

* The numbers correspond to the Twelve Steps of Alcoholics Anonymous adapted for Sexual Addicts listed on page 137.

OLD CORE BELIEFS	PROGRAM PROVISIONS FOR BOTH ADDICTS AND CO-ADDICTS

3. My needs are never going to be met if I have to depend on others.

When Program members admit their needs they have their first experience in the care of the fellowship. The Program has no conditions or restrictions. Members receive affirmation through admitting their need. The care they experience provides a basic support which allows the members to trust a Higher Power and the human community to supply the care they need and to discard the old self-destructive behaviors.

4. Sex is my most important need (addicts), or sex is the most important sign of love (co-addicts).

Addicts and co-addicts learn the power the addiction had in their lives. They discover they do not need the addiction to survive, but they do need the Program consistently because of the addiction's power. By recognizing their powerlessness and unmanageability, addicts and co-addicts start to live new lives which focus on human relationships as opposed to sex. Program members continue to learn about this process through teaching others.

148

AND CHANGING BELIEFS *(Continued)*

KEY STEPS*	NEW BELIEFS	INTEGRATED WORLD
6,7	My needs can be met by others if I let them know what I need.	By taking more responsibility for themselves, addicts and co-addicts see their roles in having their needs met. Addiction or co-addiction is unnecessary for dealing with anxiety or pain. To be dependent on others is acceptable. When disappointed, appropriate anger invites further human connection as opposed to rage which keeps others out.
10,11,12	Sex is but one expression of my need and care for others.	Addicts and co-addicts find what their obsession could never discover: a deep and personal sense of self-worth and value. They can be affirmed and loved, as well as loving and affirming. They learn that rewarding and varied sexual experience within the context of significant relationships adds nurturing to one's life. Living the Program assures them that sexual obsession does not direct their lives.

* The numbers correspond to the Twelve Steps of Alcoholics Anonymous adapted for Sexual Addicts listed on page 137.

being described. For Dan, this was the first realization that maybe the group might fit for him.

Dan attended more meetings. He listened as one man shared his First Step. He began to realize that his behavior was really not much different. The exploitation, the efforts to stop, the painful feelings afterwards and real consequences fit for him. Soon Dan asked a member of the group to be his sponsor. His sponsor was an older man who had been in the Program for about four years. Patiently, the sponsor tutored Dan about how the Steps worked. Dan was amazed at the complexity and the depth of the Twelve Steps. They were deceptive in their simplicity. Dan recognized that he had much to learn.

Also, Dan was astounded at how quickly people in the group became important to him. They listened to him for many hours on the phone, over coffee, and at lunch. Belonging to the Program meant joining up with this network of caring people which extended far beyond the one meeting a week. For the first time in his life, Dan had friends whom he could trust not to abandon him.

Dan found he was sharing parts of himself that he had not even told his therapist, although his group was quick to suggest specific issues that he should bring to therapy. The group stressed that they were not a therapy group, but a Twelve Step Program. Most group members recognized, however, that therapy and treatment were important parts of recovery.

Starting the First Step

Dan's sponsor encouraged Dan to start preparing his First Step. Preparation of the First Step involved sharing his sexual history, emphasizing how he was powerless and how his life had become unmanageable. Dan's sponsor told him that he should ask his therapist for assistance as well. "The First Step is too painful to prepare alone,'' he said. With the help of his sponsor, some group members, and his therapist, Dan started to work. In many ways, it was like preparing for a long journey. Much preparation and planning was necessary before he could start.

Dan's pilgrimage took over three weeks. It was the custom in Dan's group to present a section of the Step each week until it was finished. Some of the sharing was light and humorous. At one point, Dan observed that asking for help was extremely hard. He was the type that would go to an unfamiliar grocery store, and rather than ask where something was, would search by himself until he found it. Everyone laughed with Dan about how addicts make life so hard even in the little things. Many parts of Dan's history were very hard to share. Dan found that the most embarrassing example of his compulsivity occurred during his summer job on a farm when he was in college. He had been sexual with farm animals. As he described what he did, his voice became so soft the group strained to listen to him. Then Dan stopped and there was a period of silence. A gentle but strong voice broke the quiet, ''Dan, I've done that too.'' As he looked up, his eyes full of tears, he looked directly at the other man. There were tears in his eyes too. Dan was not alone.

The most painful part for Dan to share was about an incident that had occurred two years before Dan had joined the group. Dan had found it exhilarating to sneak into people's houses and watch women undress. He would hide in closets or under beds and then sneak out after everyone was asleep. One of his favorite homes to do this in belonged to some family friends of his parents' who had two college-age daughters. One night the mother discovered him hiding in the hall closet. He was profoundly embarrassed because his whole family as well as their friends were involved. In the aftermath, Dan was even more of an outcast in his family.

The group stopped Dan as he was describing all the events that transpired as a result of being discovered. They asked Dan how he felt at the time. He described how he just wanted to die. He acted as if he didn't care—but he was deeply humiliated. Then the group asked him how he felt now. Dan paused. He told them he was angry—angry about being an addict, angry at having to come to the group, angry that he couldn't be just like normal people, angry that he was in such a terrible situation. As the emotions continued, he talked of his sadness about all the people he had hurt, how he had never wanted to be in those situations, and how desperate he had been to stop. He recognized he was powerless—and he felt so alone. His words stopped. All that could be heard now was his deep sobbing, tears that had waited for many years.

Dan learned that night the real depths of his powerlessness—yet he also learned that he was not alone. Life was not a grocery store in which he had to search by himself. Change could occur with the help of a fellowship that cared. Yet, without help and the prerequisite admission that he faced something stronger than he was, he could make no progress.

For months after his First Step, Dan found himself flooded with insight. Other examples and events came to mind—more pieces of a larger puzzle. His group had especially helped him understand the ways he had been abused as a child. His therapist showed Dan how he could translate his new learnings into new behavior. Through his therapy and his Program, Dan was achieving a fundamental restructuring of his beliefs as well as an openness to intimacy he had never experienced before.

Even his group noted changes. One member commented to Dan that he could now ''see his teeth.'' He went on to explain that when Dan first came to the group, his smiles were very tight. Now, however, his smiles were relaxed and broad.

Dan was involved soon in his first Twelfth Step call. A Twelfth Step call is when an addict is in need of help and group members meet with the person to assist his or her entry into the Program. In this case, the person was sent to the group by the same therapist who had referred Dan. As they met over breakfast, Dan asked the man why he wanted to join the group. He responded by saying that at this point he was not sure that he belonged in the group since he did not know much about it. His therapist, however, was really insistent that he go. Dan remembered his early days and his mind was flooded with realizations about how far he himself had come.

The Impact of the First Step

Dan's experience is typical. People who enter the Program go through clear stages. The first is *denial*. Dan did not believe he needed to belong to the Program. He thought he could handle his own problems, therefore he kept having them. The second stage is *compliance*. Going through the motions does not indicate acceptance of the Program's principles. Rather, people often attend out of duty or even hope that maybe the Program might be helpful.

After a time, the new member reaches a third stage, *intellectual acceptance*. The member sees the relevance of the Program, empathizes with other members, and makes connections to his or her own behaviors. At this point, the new member starts to develop friendly relationships within the group. Once this support network is established, the member moves to the next stage of *emotional acceptance*. Like Dan, this occurs only after the member has really examined the impact the addiction has had on his life.

With that emotional acceptance, the group member experiences an internal surrender to the basic paradox of the First Step. All those years of trying to control the behavior simply intensified the problem. Giving up control, admitting you

153

cannot stop your behavior, acknowledging that this addiction is destroying your life, asking for help—are the exact opposite actions of what seems natural to do. Yet, the Step works.

Preparation of the Step

For those of you who are beginning the Program, even though you surrender, there is still work to do. Once you have accepted the Program's principles, the continuing expansion of awareness leads to a highly creative period for insight into your life. To admit the extremes of your life, and thus become totally exposed, requires a true feeling of support and concern from the group. To be accepted by others is the final rupture of the addictive system. Finally, the First Step will be repeated over and over again in your life—sometimes formally, sometimes in small ways. Each repetition may be done with greater insight, but never with less need. The First Step should be written. You should record as many *specific* examples of powerlessness and unmanageability as possible. Notes should be made of what it was like each time, including feelings, fantasies, concerns, and fears. Do not do this process alone. Share examples with your sponsor, therapist, or group members. Consulting with others builds in accountability since they can serve as a reality check. Also, these people serve as an important bridge as you sever the bonds of your double life. With their help, you do not have to be stuck in your shame as you write.

Extending your writing can be helpful. Writing in a journal, for example, can add autobiographical depth to your Step. Many treatment programs and therapists require an autobiography of addicts and co-addicts. While the First Step is not designed to deal with your whole life story, there are a number of key life experiences and persons who are very relevant to your addiction. Are there any patterns which emerge? What are the secrets you keep? Who are the significant people who have abandoned you? Recovery starts with identification. By specifying incidents, you can begin to own (to acknowledge and take responsibility for) your addiction. It may help you to reread the early chapters of this book and to review your responses to the various checklists supplied.

For addicts, special attention should be given to the last episode of sexual acting out. Think about exactly what happened, preceded, and followed the incident. What were your feelings and thoughts? If you can establish the date of the incident, that will become your "straight date." In the years to come it will be an important anniversary to mark your progress in the Program.

You also need to explore the ways you were victimized as a child or adolescent. Think of people who were inappropriately sexual with you—Who physically abused you? Who emotionally abused you? Or who neglected you? How did you think and feel at the time? In what ways were you powerless over these events?

Finally, a thorough First Step takes into account the impact of other addictive behaviors like alcoholism, compulsive eating, and workaholism. Avoid casual linkages like "my sexual behavior was the result of my drinking." Rather, note that both addictions were present at the same time. By blaming one addiction on the other, you minimize the addiction's power. By ignoring the presence of other addictions, you dismiss the totality of the addictive process and of your own pain.

Co-addicts use the same process that the addict does, but there are important differences. Obviously, co-addicts are preoccupied and obsessed with the addicts' behavior. Co-addicts have to admit powerlessness over the addicts. Co-addicts will feel angry about being connected to an addict. Abuse issues and other addictions are important factors for the co-addicts as well.

The following exercise will assist you in thinking about your addiction. You may wish to use a separate sheet or journal to complete the tasks required. The first task is to make two lists. One list should record sexual experiences in your life which have been degrading or exploitive. The other list should contain experiences which have been enriching or life-enhancing. Take care to be absolutely honest with yourself. Also make your descriptions as specific as possible.

DEGRADING OR EXPLOITIVE BEHAVIOR

1. _____

2. _____

3. _____

4. _____

5. _____

6. _____

7. _____

8. _____

WORKSHEET

Now note the common feelings, attitudes, and situations in each list. For example, did the activities in the first list involve secrecy or dishonesty? How are they different? What guidelines do the lists indicate in terms of addictive behavior which you need to stop? Share these with someone who understands your Program (i.e., a sponsor, therapist, or group member).

ENRICHING OR LIFE-ENHANCING BEHAVIOR

1. _____

_____

2. _____

_____

3. _____

_____

4. _____

_____

5. _____

_____

6. _____

_____

7. _____

_____

8. _____

_____

Many addicts and co-addicts find that professional assistance accelerates recovery. Treatment programs and therapists offer a number of advantages. First, if they are skilled in addiction and knowledgeable in the Twelve Step Program, they can help you focus on the fundamental changes necessary to arrest your illness. Second, professionals can assist families in restructuring their relationships with skills and perspectives in addition to what the Twelve Steps offer. Finally, they can attend to the mental health issues which are often concurrent with the addiction.

The SAFE Formula

Unlike an alcoholic who can abstain and maintain sobriety, the sexual addict has to face the fact of his or her own sexuality. Like the overeater, recovery does not mean the elimination of fundamental human processes. Celibacy does not resolve the problem. The question emerges for addicts as to how they determine when their sexual behavior is addictive.

The following formula is suggested as a guideline. Signs of compulsive sexuality are when the behavior can be described as follows:

1. It is a *Secret*. Anything that cannot pass public scrutiny will create the shame of a double life.
2. It is *Abusive* to self or others. Anything that is exploitive or harmful to others or degrades oneself will activate the addictive system.
3. It is used to avoid or is a source of painful *Feelings*. If sexuality is used to alter moods or results in painful mood shifts, it is clearly part of the addictive process.
4. It is *Empty* of a caring, committed relationship. Fundamental to the whole concept of addiction and recovery is

the healthy dimension of human relationships. The addict runs a great risk by being sexual outside of a committed relationship.

The advantage of the SAFE (Secret, Abusive, Feelings, Empty) formula is that it is built on the basic concept of addiction and is in the spirit of the Twelve Steps. It requires a ruthless honesty given that the addict's sanity is at stake. Using the group or a sponsor as an on-going reality check can help keep the addict "safe." You may wish to use "The Addict's Worksheet" on pages 156 and 157 as a means for thinking about your own behavior.

Joining a Group

Seeking a Twelve Step group feels difficult, because by searching you admit you have a problem. Start by checking local community referral agencies or phone services. Private therapists, pastors, social service agencies, and Alcoholics Anonymous and Al-Anon programs (for family members of alcoholics) are also good resources. You may even be fortunate to have a treatment program in your area. Many local alcoholism programs are now offering help for sexual addicts. Then you could join a Twelve Step group after you have finished treatment.

Some cities as well as rural areas have a large number of groups—including groups for family members and women addicts. If that is true in your area, remember that each group has its own unique character. Some have a style or composition that may not be a good match for you, so continue searching. However, remember the six-meeting rule, because the problem may not be with the group but with your denial.

If you become discouraged, find a copy of the "Big Book" of Alcoholics Anonymous. Read the first eleven chapters which tell of the early days of AA in the late 1930s when AA had less than a hundred members. Look specifically at chapter five, "How It Works," which says in part:

> Rarely have we seen a person fail who has thoroughly followed our path. Those who do not recover are people who cannot or will not completely give themselves to this simple program, usually men and women who are constitutionally incapable of being honest with themselves...Many of us exclaimed, "What an order! I can't go through with it." Do not be discouraged. No one among us has been able to maintain anything like perfect adherence to these principles. We are not saints. The point is that we are willing to grow along spiritual lines.

7

The Future Is Conditional

I am larger, better than I thought.
I did not know I held so much goodness.

Walt Whitman

John was a town councilman. He had been an effective and well-liked leader. John was also a sexual addict, but had received treatment and been in a Twelve Step Program for two years. A newspaper reporter had dug up an old police report that John had been accused of exposing himself. The reporter described the accusation in an article which quickly brought demands for John's resignation. When John resigned, an outstanding community member appointed by the council replaced him. The irony was that John's replacement was from his own Twelve Step group.

A second story relates the experience of the school teacher who was sexual with students. When the facts became known, the community stood behind the teacher. He had made an enormous contribution to the welfare of the town. Townspeople sensitively stood behind the teacher, helped him get treatment, and kept his job open.

The contrast in public attitudes is obvious. Unfortunately, most people react as the townspeople did in John's case. Part of the problem is that for the public to understand the sexual addiction, the majority would have to conduct painful self-appraisals of their own beliefs and family rules. Because of the many social factors, professionals can only guess at the extent of sexual compulsivity. Addicts simply do not volunteer that information. Nor is there public pride in recovery. A sex addict cannot, in our day and time, proudly announce his or her recovery—as alcoholics now can.

Sexual addicts need to remember the decades of struggle that alcoholics had to go through in order to earn public acceptance of their illness. Even now large parts of the population still see alcoholism as a matter of moral degeneracy. We are perhaps decades away from a public understanding of the problem of sexual addiction. The surest way to gain the public support will be to document the cost—the cost to addicts, their families, the community, business and industry.

A military chaplain describes a situation which illustrates the cost. On an overseas base, one man's sexual binges had a serious impact on his work. He contracted a particularly vicious form of venereal disease seventeen times during a two-year tour. When the situation was brought to the attention of the base commander, his response was that he could not act on something that was so clearly a personal matter. The chaplain pointed out that the venereal disease was so severe each time that the man had lost on the average of four days of work per treatment. The base commander understood the chaplain's point. Together they worked with the man to get him to the help he needed.

The sexual addiction affects job productivity and performance. Distraction, time loss, unmanageability, poor decision-making—all are commonly reported by addicts. Each addict's story, however, makes a unique statement about the cost:

- the manager of a large retail outlet who was fired when he completed a two-month term in jail for incest.
- the bank executive who discovered during treatment that his job promotion had been held back for years because of his sexual addiction.
- the laid-off truck driver who sold food stamps on the black market to buy gas in order to cruise eight to sixteen hours daily looking for women.

- the cab driver with seven children who could not renew his license due to an arrest for sexual misconduct.
- the child advocate who had to confess child abuse.
- the beauty shop owner who lost his business because of involvement with clients.
- the owner of a family appliance business who lost his wife and his business because of incest.
- the forty-five-year-old painter who spent a total of twenty-five years in prison for various sex-related charges.
- the nursing home attendant who requested not to work with female patients because of his fears of obsession.

Employers have a special perspective on the costs of sexual addiction. They can see the patterns. The bishop who has to move yet again a young clergyman who has a habit of being sexual with parishioners, the superintendent who hears still another story about the seventh grade math teacher who masturbates in the classroom, and the executive whose firm faces a sexual harassment suit against one of his employees because of his sexual behavior—all have in common the perspective of an emerging pattern of sexual addiction. They also can put pressure on the addict to seek help.

Procedures that are now routine for intervening with alcoholics in most professional, business, and industrial settings can be utilized for the sexual addict as well. Already many employee assistance programs are recognizing that there are valuable, talented people who cannot help themselves because of their illness. In fact, many of the alcoholism programs are developing special tracks for sexual compulsiveness to respond to industry's need. This is especially appropriate given that many suffer from both sexual addiction and addiction to alcohol and/or other drugs.

The addict can be helped in many ways, including:

- public awareness of the sexual addiction as a tragic illness which can be stopped in most cases.

- elimination of jokes which degrade people's struggle with their sexual compulsivity, i.e., "flasher" jokes, dirty bookstore jokes.
- support by local community agencies including churches, schools, and hospitals to allow meetings in their facilities.
- honest appraisal of the problem by judges so that treatment is one of the consequences.
- prevention programs which promote family health and communication, especially about sexual issues.
- treatment providers who extend services not only to the addicts, but family members as well.
- clinicians who are not bound by narrow categories so they miss the overall picture, including the interconnectedness, of compulsive behavior.
- lawyers, ministers, and physicians who can see the signs of the addiction and can intervene in the destructive cycle.
- police who neither dismiss nor overreact to the addict's problem.
- alcoholism counselors who are willing to apply their special skills to multiple addictions.
- child protection workers who recognize that all members of the family are desperate.
- researchers who, using critical scientific standards, take on the difficult task of expanding understanding.

By making these efforts to help sexual addicts and co-addicts, we can support the spirit of the Twelve Step Program. If this book contributes towards that end, it will have accomplished its purpose: to create legitimacy for those courageous people who wish to face their sexual compulsivity for what it truly is—an addiction. With our help, those addicts will be truly able to say, in the words of Walt Whitman,

> I am larger, better than I thought.
> I did not know I held so much goodness.

References

Chapter One

1. MacAuliffe, M., and MacAuliffe, R., *The Essentials of Chemical Dependency,* Minneapolis: American Chemical Dependency Society, 1975.

2. The concept of concurrent addictions is being more widely accepted. William Miller, for example, writes, "What do the following have in common: alcoholism, obesity, smoking, drug abuse, and compulsive gambling? Until a few years ago, these were thought of as relatively independent and separate problem areas. Psychologists, psychiatrists, social workers, and other mental health professionals have often specialized in the treatment of one of these behaviors, but few have extended their therapy and research efforts to cover more than one or two of these disorders. In addition, specialists in each of these areas have worked in relative isolation from one another, seldom communicating with each other about treatment and research issues. The past few years, however, have witnessed a remarkable amount of growth and change in professional knowledge within these areas. The emergent concept of 'the addictive behaviors' points to possible commonalities among these seemingly diverse problems." William R. Miller, *The Addictive Behaviors* (New York, N.Y., Pergamon Press, 1980).
   For the professional, a useful journal committed to this subject is *Addictive Diseases: An International Journal,* Spectrum Publications 75-31, 192nd St., Flushing, N.Y.

3. For a description of the literature describing the interaction of drugs, alcohol, and sexual compulsivity, see *Contrary to*

Love, Understanding Sexual Addiction, Part 2: Helping the Sexual Addict, the companion volume to this book (Comp-Care Publishers, in press).

4. Professionals need to read *Contrary to Love, Understanding Sexual Addiction, Part 2: Helping the Sexual Addict,* about diagnostic indicators of this problem.

5. For an excellent summary of this literature, see: "Group Approaches to Counseling," by Warren Shaffer and Alan Anderson, chapter eight of the *Handbook of Counseling Psychology* (John Wiley, in press).

Chapter Two

1. For readers who wish to read further on sexual behavior during phases of transition, see:

   Sheehy, Gail, *Passages: Predictable Crises in Adult Life,* New York: E.P. Dutton & Co., 1974.
   Weiss, Robert S., *Marital Separation,* New York: Basic Books, Inc., 1975.
   Reed, David M., "Sexual Behavior in the Separated, Divorced, and Widowed," in *The Sexual Experience,* editors Sadock, Kaplan, and Freedman, Baltimore: Williams and Wilkins Co., 1976.
   Blos, Peter, *The Adolescent Passage,* New York: International Universities Press, Inc., 1979.

2. An example of the prevailing belief is a statement from Lt. Jim Bullard's *Looking Forward to Being Attached* (Memphis Police Department). "Exhibitionists generally are introverted and shy. They are bashful. They are almost never dangerous."

3. From an unpublished manuscript presented at the First Annual Conference for the Treatment of Sexual Aggressives, July, 1977.

4. Malamuth, Neil, "Rapists and Normal Men," *Treatment for Sexual Aggressives News,* 1982, 5:1.

5. MacNamara, Donald E. and Sagarin, Edward, *Sex, Crime, and the Law,* New York: The Free Press, 1978.

6. For a review of literature on this subject, see *Contrary to Love, Understanding Sexual Addiction, Part 2: Helping the Sexual Addict,* by this author (CompCare Publishers, in press).

Chapter Three

1. Coleman, Nick, "Brothers Sentenced in Sex Case," *Minneapolis Tribune,* January 20, 1982.

2. Eist, H., and Mandel, A., "Family Treatment of On-going Incest Behavior," *Family Process,* 1968, 7:216.

3. Sherman, Julia, "The Coatlicue Complex: A Source of Irrational Reactions Against Women," *Transactional Analysis Journal,* 1975, 5:2.

Chapter Five

1. Lewis, Helen Block, *Psychic War in Men and Women,* New York: New York University Press, 1976.

2. Farrell, Warren, "We Teach Men to be Rapists," *Sexuality Today,* 1978, 1:32, p.3.

3. May, Rollo, *Power and Innocence: A Search for the Sources of Innocence*, New York: W. W. Norton & Co., Inc., 1972.

4. Bandler, Richard and Grinder, John, *The Structure of Magic*, vols. 1 and 2, Palo Alto, CA: Science and Behavior Books, 1975.

Chapter Six

1. Boodman, Sandra, "Former Educator Sentenced to Jail," *Washington Post*, April 28, 1982, p. C11, col. 1.

2. Becker, Ernest, *The Denial of Death*, New York: The Free Press, 1973.

Resource Guide

Perhaps the best source for general information on sex addiction is the National Council on Sex Addiction, P.O. Box 20249, Wickenburg, Arizona 85358 (telephone 602-684-7919). In addition, individual fellowships publish literature and periodicals. A list is provided at the conclusion of this guide.

For professional clinicians, *Professional's Guide to Resources in Treatment of Sexual Addiction* may be obtained by contacting the Sexual Dependency Unit, Del Amo Hospital, 23700 Camino Del Sol, Torrance, California 90505, or call 310-530-1151 or 1-800-5DELAMO. A special Sexual Addiction Hotline for emergencies, consultations, and referrals is also available: call 800-551-9888.

For sex addicts, *Hope and Recovery, A Twelve Step Guide for Healing from Compulsive Sexual Behavior* (CompCare, 1987) has long been a useful guide. It is now also available in workbook form (*Hope and Recovery, The Workbook*, CompCare, 1991). A new effort by Patrick Carnes is *Don't Call It Love* (Bantam, 1991), which resulted from a four-year study of a thousand recovering sex addicts. Other contributions are Anne Wilson Schaef's highly readable *Escape from Intimacy* (Harper and Row, 1989) and Ralph Earle's powerful *Lonely All the Time* (PB 1990). *What Everyone Needs to Know about Sex Addiction* (CompCare, 1989) includes first-person stories by a sex addict and a codependent. Add Charlotte Kasl's important book *Women, Sex, and Addiction* (HarperCollins, 1990), and Jed Diamond's *Looking for Love in All the Wrong Places* (Avon, 1989), and we find a complete bookshelf being created for recovering sex addicts.

For survivors of sexual abuse, many new resources have appeared. Mic Hunter's *Abused Boys* (Lexington Books, 1989) is a groundbreaking effort to create resources for men who were abused. Wendy Maltz, whose *Incest and Sexuality* (Lexington Books, 1987) is already regarded as a classic, is also the author of *The Sexual Healing Journey* (HarperCollins, 1991). It is superb, her best effort so far. It provides concrete ways for a victim to reintegrate the sexual self. Similarly, Ellen Bass and Laura Davis have created classics in their *Courage to Heal* (Harper and Row, 1988), book and workbook. Their new book, *Allies in Healing* (HarperCollins, 1991), is extremely well-crafted and fills an important gap as a resource for the spouse of a survivor. *Growing Beyond Abuse* (Omni Recovery, Inc., 1990), a workbook by Signe L. Nestingen and Laurel Ruth Davis, provides an effective tool for healing from sexual exploitation by therapists, as well as from childhood abuse. Probably one of the most important books in this category is Dr. Patricia Love's *Emotional Incest Syndrome* (Bantam, 1990). This book has been an eye-opener for many.

For adult children of alcoholics and other addictions, the sexual issues are legion. A fine guide to integrating recovery and sexuality is *Aching for Love: The Sexual Drama of the Adult Child* by Mary A. Klausner and Bobbie Hasselbring (Harper San Francisco, 1990). Claudia Black's *Double Duty* (MAC Publishing, 1990), is very helpful about sexual issues, as well as others. For women, Stephanie Covington has written an excellent guide called *Awakening Your Sexuality* (Harper San Francisco, 1991).

For family members of sex addicts, Jennifer Schneider has added to her wonderful book *Back from Betrayal* (Hazelden, 1989), a new book entitled *Sex, Lies, and Forgiveness* (HarperCollins, 1991), which is based on systematic interviews of recovering couples. Dr. Schneider continues to be an inspiration to recovering family members. *The First Step for People in Relationships with Sex Addicts* (CompCare, 1989) by Mic Hunter and "Jem," presents a question-and-answer format that addresses the addict and the codependent person who becomes a part of the disease. A new book, *If My Dad's a Sexaholic, What Does That Make Me?*, by Barbara LairRobinson and Rick LairRobinson (CompCare, 1991) raises the whole issue of being an adult child of a sex addict.

On intimacy issues as they affect sexual behavior, two highly regarded and useful books are Harriet Goldhor Lerner's *Dance of Intimacy* (Harper and Row, 1988) and *The Dance of Anger* (Harper and Row, 1985). I also like John H. Driggs and Stephen E. Finn's *Intimacy Between Men: How to Find and Keep Gay Love Relationships* (Dutton, 1990) for homosexuality and intimacy.

A task for many clients is resolving issues in the family, especially sexual ones. *Dear Dad* (Viking Penguin, 1989) by Louie Anderson is a good model for the courage it takes. John Bradshaw's *Homecoming* (Bantam, 1990) is filled with strategies for resolution of family of origin issues and is a testimony to the possibilities of the human spirit. Melody Beattie's *The Language of Letting Go* (Harper/Hazelden, 1990) is a gentle way to personal resolution. For journaling strategies, no better book exists than Christina Baldwin's *Life's Companion: Journal Writing as a Spiritual Quest* (Bantam, 1991).

Facing Shame (Norton, 1986) by Merle Fossum and Marilyn Mason was intended for therapists and is one of the best books available on family therapy and addictions. It is highly readable, however, and most readers will find it filled with extraordinary insight on family functioning.

A final suggestion: in many ways therapy and recovery are like reparenting, wherein we are adding new voices to supplant the old destructive ones. Good books can add new messages plus empower you to be able to affirm your sexuality from within. Sharing reading with your partner and in your groups can only add to your understanding and intimacy. The gift of recovery means we no longer have to do things in isolation.

To arrange for seminars, conferences, workshops, or lectures by Patrick Carnes, call 612-782-0510.

Twelve Step Fellowships

Fellowship

Sex Addicts Anonymous (SAA)
P.O. Box 3038
Minneapolis, MN 55403
(612) 871-1520, (612) 339-0217

Sex and Love Addicts Anonymous (SLAA)
P.O. Box 119
New Town Branch
Boston, MA 02258
(617) 332-1845

Sexaholics Anonymous (SA)
P.O. Box 300
Simi Valley, CA 93062
(805) 581-3343

Sexual Compulsives Anonymous (SCA)
  West Coast:
    P.O. Box 4470
    170 Sunset Blvd. #520
    Los Angeles, CA 90027
    (310) 859-5585
  East Coast:
    P.O. Box 1585
    Old Chelsea Station
    New York, New York 10011
    (212) 439-1123

Publications

The Plain Brown Rapper
(Contact SAA)

The Journal
(Contact SLAA)

Essay
(Contact SA)

The Scanner
(Contact West Coast)

Co-Sex and Love Addicts Anonymous (COSA)
P.O. Box 14537
Minneapolis, MN 55414
(612) 537-6904

S-Anon Family Groups
P.O. Office 5117
Sherman Oaks, CA 91413
(818) 990-6910

Adults Anonymous Molested as Children
AAMAC World Services Organization
P.O. Box 662
Apple Valley, CA 92307

About the Author

Patrick J. Carnes, Ph.D., C.A.S., is the clinical director of new programs for sexual addiction and trauma treatment at Del Amo Hospital in Torrance, California. Dr. Carnes is a nationally known speaker on addiction and recovery issues, as well as the author of four books on addiction: *Out of the Shadows,* Understanding Sexual Addiction (1983); *Contrary to Love,* Helping the Sexual Addict (1989); *A Gentle Path through the Twelve Steps,* For All People in the Process of Recovery (1989) all from CompCare Publishers; and *Don't Call It Love,* Recovery from Sexual Addiction (1991) from Bantam Books. Additionally, Dr. Carnes serves on the National Advisory Board of the American Academy of Health Care Providers in the Addictive Disorders – a national certification organization for clinical professionals. Dr. Carnes is the focus of a twelve-part PBS series called "Contrary to Love," a series on addictions. The show continues to air on Public Broadcasting Systems across the country.

Previously, Dr. Carnes designed and created the country's first inpatient sexual dependency facility at Golden Valley Health Center in Minneapolis. He was a founding board member of the National Council on Sex Addiction (NCSA), a community and professional organization for public awareness about sexual health.

Carnes, who lives in Minneapolis, received his doctorate in education and counseling from the University of Minnesota.

Index

Arrests. *See also* Legal Sanctions
  and belief system, 6-7
  and unmanageability, 12
Assumptions in addictive system,
  14. *See also* Myths

B
Barriers against scrutiny, 98
Behavior. *See also* Recovery
  controlling, in co-addiction,
    96-97
  in levels of addiction, 54-55
  and other addictions, 60
  as recovery issue, 24
  shifting of, 56
  and studies, 56
Belief system
  as addiction support, vii
  chart of core beliefs, 81-85
  chart of male addict's, 120-121
  core belief #1, 138-140
  core belief #2, 140-142
  core belief #3, 142-143
  core belief #4, 143-145
  core beliefs #5-6, 127-132
  core and addict, 77-81
  cultural, 115-122
  family, 122-127
  and impaired thinking, 6-9
  and recovery, 19-21
  restructure, need to, 24
  as world model, 5
Bill's story, 49-51
Bingeing
  and exhibitionism, 43
  sexual, 24-26
Blame
  in co-addiction, 75-96
  dynamic of, 8

C
Centerfolds, 31-33
Cermak case, 63-64
Change, vowing to. *See* Delusion
Chemical dependency. *See also*
  Alcoholism
  link to sexual compulsivity, i
Child molesting. *See also* Abuse;
  Incest
  Cermak case, 63-64
  in level three, 45-46
  in levels of addiction, 54-55
Choices, making. *See also* Belief
  System
  and beliefs, 5
Circular reasoning in impaired
  thinking, 7
Co-addiction, 87-113
  addict's, 120-121
  checklist, 100-101
  as family illness, 108-109
  secrecy in, 97-98
  system in, 93-99
  world of co-addict, 110-113
Coe story, 87-93
Compulsion (compulsivity)
  in addictive system, 14-18
  in family system, ii
  and loss from, xi
  periods of, 25
  rape as part of pattern, 47
  and sexual behavior, 9-12
Conquests, excitement of, 10
Consequences, v. *See also* Arrests;
  Belief System; Legal Sanctions
  and addiction, 24-26
  and belief system, 6-8
  and escalation of addiction, 27
  outside addiction, 25
  vulnerability to, 4

F

Family. *See also* Marital
  Relationship; Myths
    coping patterns of, ii
    danger in, 2-3
    involvement in therapy, 49
    isolation of, ix
    role of, 65-76
    runaways, 65-67
    and sexual addiction as lifestyle,
      64
    systems and addiction, ii, viii
Family Renewal Center, i-ii
Fantasy in sexual addiction, 2-5
Fear and recovery, 20
First Step
    beginning, 150-153
    impact of, 153-154
    preparation for, xi, 154-158
    worksheet, 156-157
Flashpoints for addiction, 13
Flashers. *See* Exhibitionism
Forgiveness, x
Fourth Step, xi
Future, a hopeful, 161-164

G

Gamblers Anonymous, 20
Gambling and sexual addiction,
  18-19, 60
George's story, 47-48
Gender and addiction, 56-59
General systems theory and family
  treatment, i-ii
Generations, role of, viii
    in addiction, 65-67
    in incest, 46
Grandiosity, 95
Grief, 88-93

H

Heterosexual relationships. *See*
  Relationships
Homosexuality in level one, 35-36,
  54-55
Honesty in recovery, 49. *See also*
  Recovery
Humiliation, 69-70
Hustler, intoxication of, 10

I

Illicit
    excitement of, 25
    indecent liberties, 44
Image. *See also* Self-image
    public, 11
    self, 17, 67-70
Inadequacy in co-addiction, 95
Incest. *See also* Child Molesting
    in level three, 45-46
    in levels of addiction, 54-55
    intoxication of forbidden, 10
Indecent
    incidents in levels of addiction,
      54-55
    liberties, 44-45, 54-55
    phone calls, 44-45
Intimacy, diminishing, vii
Intoxication, of sex, 10
Isolation, ix
    of double life, 13-14
"Itch" of addiction, vii

J

Jim's story, 35-36
Jobs. *See also* Work
    in addictive system, 14
    and belief system, 6-9
    loss of, 44

An Excerpt from
the Revised Edition of
A Gentle Path through the Twelve Steps:
The Classic Guide for All People in
the Process of Recovery
by Patrick Carnes, Ph.D.

Sharing Your First Step

You have not fully taken your First Step unless you have shared it with others. One Twelve Step group has a tradition that, after ninety days in the program, a newcomer shares his or her first Step. The expectation helps remove procrastination. If you do a First Step in treatment, you may wish to do it again with your Twelve Step group. When you share your First Step, usually with a group, focus on telling about the depth and pain of your powerlessness, not necessarily your whole story. Choose incidents that are most moving to you. Get feedback and support from your guides about what to share. Remember, your goal is not to perform for others, but to help you see and accept your powerlessness. The more honest you are, the more relief you will feel.

The First Step invites you to share freely, holding little back. This is called "taking a Step" and means a fundamental acknowledgment of the illness and a surrender to a different life. Some people go through the motions of a First

Excerpt from the revised edition of *A Gentle Path through the Twelve Steps:The Classic Guide for All People in the Process of Recovery* by Patrick Carnes, Ph.D.

Step without actually taking the Step. They avoid the Step by sharing examples of their powerlessness and unmanageability, as if they are unrelated: They are detached from the impact of their illness. Taking the Step means clearly admitting the patterns of the illness and sharing the feelings that accompany the realization that you have been out of control. Healing occurs only when the Step goes past intellectual acceptance to emotional surrender.

Here's a comparison of some of the characteristics of *taking* versus *avoiding* a Step:

Taking a Step	Avoiding a Step
Deliberate	Speedy
Thoughtful	Just reporting
Emotionally present	Emotionally absent
Feelings congruent with reality	Absence of feelings
Statements of ownership of feelings and responsibility for behavior	Blame, denial, projection
Events form patterns	Events seem isolated
Acceptance	Defensiveness
Acknowledge impact	Deny impact

Excerpt from the revised edition of *A Gentle Path through the Twelve Steps:The Classic Guide for All People in the Process of Recovery* by Patrick Carnes, Ph.D.

Surrender to illness	Attempt to limit illness
See addiction as part of life	See addiction as something to be fixed

---

Be aware of the tendency to become detached when telling your story. Try to remain open to both your own feelings and the group with whom you are sharing.

There are many reasons why people avoid, sometimes indefinitely, taking their First Step. Read the following items and see if any apply to you:

Failure of courage To face an illness requires great courage. Some people are unable or unwilling to do it. If you find yourself thinking that you don't really need to do anything or that you can handle it by yourself, find someone in the program to support you in your fearful moments.

Not witnessing a good First Step If you have never seen a First Step taken, then you have no real model of what to do. Watch someone else take the First Step, or ask your guide to talk to you about his or her First Step—how it was taken, what it meant.

Inadequate preparation If you have not carefully prepared and consulted with your guides—that is, if you haven't carefully examined your own story— do not proceed. A First Step is not something you can do hastily.

Excerpt from the revised edition of *A Gentle Path through the Twelve Steps:The Classic Guide for All People in the Process of Recovery* by Patrick Carnes, Ph.D.

Denial of impact If you find yourself minimizing ("Things were not so bad") or wondering if you are making something out of nothing, it's time to go back over your story with your guides.

Acting out Actively holding on to some aspect of the addiction or coaddiction, even in some very small way, will interfere with taking your First Step. Remember, you will not feel better until you completely stop your compulsive behavior.

Holding on to a major secret Secrets most often involve shame, and shame will serve as a barrier to the self-acceptance necessary in taking a First Step. Share the secret with your guides or therapist before proceeding.

Distrust of group Having confidence in your group is necessary in order for you to take the risks for your First Step work. If you do not feel comfortable in the group, talk to your guides about your options.

Inadequate understanding of the Twelve Step program When you were brought into the program, someone explained how the Steps work. Each Step has a special purpose; all Twelve Steps taken in order will lead you to recovery. If you are still confused about the program, seek some help before attempting your Step work.

The concept of the "addictive personality shift" will help you here. Addicts and coaddicts acknowledge that in their illness, it seems like there are two people inside them—the real person who tries to live up to values and cares about people, and another per-

Excerpt from the revised edition of *A Gentle Path through the Twelve Steps:The Classic Guide for All People in the Process of Recovery* by Patrick Carnes, Ph.D.

son whose values and relationships are sacrificed to addictive obsession. This Jekyll-Hyde experience is very common. The addict within us all is, in the words of the "Big Book" of Alcoholics Anonymous, "cunning and baffling." Even being able to recognize the shift from when you are your true self and when your addict has taken over is an extremely helpful tool for detaching from your addict's power.

In terms of your First Step, your addict within will work hard to sabotage your efforts at an open sharing of your illness. List below five ways your addict might try to interfere with your First Step.

Example: Rationalization—"When I was drinking, my boss loved my work."

1. _____

2. _____

3. _____

4. _____

5. _____

Sharing your Step work is crucial throughout the program.

Excerpt from the revised edition of *A Gentle Path through the Twelve Steps: The Classic Guide for All People in the Process of Recovery* by Patrick Carnes, Ph.D.

An Excerpt from
*Hope And Recovery: A Twelve
Step Guide for Healing from
Compulsive Sexual Behavior*
by Anonymous

Am I Really Out of Control?

"Sex Addict"—the words conjured up terrible images in our minds and reminded us of other words like "sick," "pervert," and "fiend." Most of us agree that the fear of being labeled sex addicts made us very reluctant to examine our sexual behaviors. But the Twelve Steps address this common fear directly. Note that the First Step begins with the word *We*; the words reassure us that others know what we have suffered and that the cause of our suffering and desperation can be identified.

When we understood and accepted the words "sex addict," we also gained new insights about our thoughts and behaviors. We learned that we were not hopelessly demented, wicked, or forever damned; *we were addicts.* And as sex addicts, we were people who continued to act out sexually, even as our lives continued to be negatively affected by our sexual behaviors. Much to our relief, we learned that addiction is not a symptom of weak will power or a lack of self-discipline. Indeed, many of us evidenced

Excerpt from *Hope and Recovery: A Twelve Step Guide for Healing from Compulsive Sexual Behavior* by Anonymous

great self-discipline and will power in other areas of our lives. But we came to see that trying to control sex addiction with will power is like trying to *think away a broken leg.* Try as we might and however good our intentions, will power is just not effective in dealing with the complex problem of sex addiction. *Besides, most of us had unsuccessfully tried to use our will power to fight our sex addiction many times.*

The use of the pronoun *We* in the First Step also reinforces the fact that addicts cannot recover alone. Addicts need the help of other addicts in order to stop their acting-out behaviors. We learned through experience that when it came to dealing with our sex addiction we were powerless as individuals, but that as a fellowship we had power. Our addiction had isolated us from other people emotionally, if not physically. But we came to understand that in order to recover, we had to be with other people and share with them.

We also learned not to confuse our admission/acknowledgment that we were powerless with the sense of being fundamentally bad people. Instead, our admission is merely a statement that we understand our problem realistically. We believe that "admitted" is another way of saying that we are aware of or have conceded the truth. *Essentially, we had to surrender to something more powerful than ourselves.* Continuing on with our fight would have brought certain destruction. For many of us, our choices finally came down to: incarceration,

Excerpt from *Hope and Recovery: A Twelve Step Guide for Healing from Compulsive Sexual Behavior* by Anonymous

insanity, or untimely death from disease, homicide, or suicide. But the Program taught us that we had another choice as well: *surrender and subsequent recovery.* We learned that there was absolutely *no reason* to be ashamed of wanting to change our lives and make them better.

The process involved in gaining new insights about ourselves and our addiction was painful. For so long, our acting-out behaviors had successfully helped us avoid or numb our feelings. We learned that acting-out was, for us, *any* sexual behavior or obsessive thinking that we engaged in to deny our feelings or distract ourselves from our feelings. Some of us came to see, for example, that even if we cruised for six hours and *did not* pick up a sex partner, we were still acting out— that our compulsive cruising was an acting-out behavior in and of itself because of the way we used it. When we began the First Step process by carefully looking at our thought and behavior patterns, some of us were able to see for the first time the hurt, loneliness, guilt, and shame that we had so desperately tried to avoid or deny. Many of us attempted to escape these insights by returning to addictive thinking. But we learned that this was only another sign that we needed to have other addicts around us during our First Step work. We need these people around to help deter us from acting out in reaction to the pain of our insights.

Excerpt from *Hope and Recovery: A Twelve Step Guide for Healing from Compulsive Sexual Behavior* by Anonymous

An Excerpt from
Contrary to Love:
Helping the Sexual Addict
by Patrick Carnes, Ph.D.

Sexual Addiction
An Overview

At a southern university medical school, a staff sexologist saw her first clients of the day. Dan and Lauren, in their late thirties, hadn't had sex in three years. During a series of sessions, other issues affecting their lives together had emerged. Lauren's resistance to Dan's sexual approaches had roots deep in addictive and abusive patterns. Sexually abused as a child, she had had several bouts with anorexia over the years. Dan was chemically dependent and had been compulsively having affairs and visiting prostitutes. The therapist diagnosed him as having a sexual addiction. Their case was familiar to her; she often found that sexual addiction coexisted with one partner's inhibited sexual desires, in the midst of a dysfunctional family system that enabled multiple addictions.

When Dan and Lauren were asked to complete a "genogram" of their families, some important background information came to light. Two of Dan's brothers were chemically dependent; one boasted a massive pornography collection. Ironically, Dan's father was a Baptist minister, well known for preaching against pornography and alcohol. Dan's paternal grandfather was a notorious womanizer and alcoholic.

Excerpt from *Contrary to Love: Helping the Sexual Addict* by Patrick Carnes, Ph.D.

To complete the picture, his grandmother had been married four times and at one time was a working prostitute. Lauren's father was an overweight, alcoholic physician who several times had been charged with the sexual abuse of patients. Her uncle had recently joined a Sexual Addicts Anonymous group in a nearby city.

While such revelations made the session painful, the genogram had done what it always does. The clients developed a clearer picture of their family history and of the role addiction played in their lives. They weren't bad people; rather they had an illness that affected the whole family. As the therapist watched the couple walk to their car, she reflected on the fact that knowing each person's dysfunction had not been sufficient to make an accurate diagnosis. The family was the missing link. She wondered how many patients she had treated with futile results before understanding the family connection.

Similiar professional soul-searching was going on in a treatment facility for impaired physicians where the director had just secured a bed in the inpatient sexual addiction unit for Phillip, a forty-two-year-old family practice physician. This was the third time he had been admitted for alcohol and drug addiction. In both of the earlier treatments, serious sexual problems had also been identified, including multiple affairs and the sexual abuse of patients. However, the loss of his license and practice was initiated by nurses' charges of sexual harassment, not the abuse of patients.

Excerpt from *Contrary to Love: Helping the Sexual Addict* by Patrick Carnes, Ph.D.